THE TEACH YOURSELF BOOKS

STAMP COLLECTING

TEACH YOURSELF
STAMP
COLLECTING

By
FRED. J. MELVILLE

Revised and brought up-to-date by
CHARLES SKILTON

THE ENGLISH UNIVERSITIES PRESS LTD
ST PAUL'S HOUSE, WARWICK LANE
LONDON EC4

First Printed	.	.	.	*1949*
Second Edition		.	.	*1961*
Third Edition	.	.	.	*1963*
Fourth Edition	.	.	.	*1968*

SBN 340 05725 4

PRINTED AND BOUND IN ENGLAND
FOR THE ENGLISH UNIVERSITIES PRESS LTD
BY HAZELL WATSON AND VINEY LTD, AYLESBURY

PREFACE

STAMP COLLECTING today is far removed from the artless game of filling up ruled spaces in a printed book. It has developed in many directions, cultural, artistic, and technical. It opens a wide outlook on a world in which international affairs have become immensely important to the understanding of the peoples as well as their governments.

It has been a mystery to non-collectors that postage stamps, old or new, weave so binding a spell upon those who collect and study them.

What is there about stamps that marks them out among so many unconsidered trifles for our interest and allurement? That they do captivate at all ages is plain from the vast numbers who collect stamps in all parts of the world.

The mystery is not to be explained in a sentence. In this book I have endeavoured to show the appeals of the stamp to different minds. I have also striven to give collectors a readable book of agreeable information, combined with a handy reference volume on most subjects that come within the purview of the Modern Stamp Collector or Philatelist.

F. J. M.

EDITOR'S NOTE

WHEN the doyen of philatelic journalists, Fred. J. Melville, died in January 1940 the world of stamp collecting suffered a great loss. His very readable books and articles had been helping to popularise the hobby for many years, and his work in founding the Junior Philatelic Society was also of tremendous value to this end.

Mr. Melville's last and greatest book, *Modern Stamp Collecting*, was published posthumously on the centenary of the first postage stamps, May 6th, 1940. It was a happy thought of the publishers to reissue this work in their famous series as *Teach Yourself Stamp Collecting*, and thus make it available to a far larger audience, and especially to the many beginners who were always Fred. J. Melville's especial interest. In revising it for this purpose I have endeavoured to retain as much as possible of the text and the spirit of the original, which I had the privilege of seeing through the press.

Acknowledgment is again made to the following firms and individuals for the loan of stamps and illustrations:

H. R. Harmer, Esq., Harmer Rooke & Co., Ltd., Bridger & Kay, Ltd., Stanley Gibbons, Ltd., Frank Godden, Ltd., H. F. Johnson, Esq., Whitfield King & Co., Robson Lowe, Esq., Chas. Nissen & Co., Ltd., R. Roberts, Esq.

Major S. H. L. Key carried out the explanatory diagrams in the text and Mr. Horace E. Coulson mounted the plates of the original edition.

CHARLES SKILTON.

CONTENTS

CONTENTS

PART III
THE STUDY OF STAMPS

LIST OF PLATES

PART I

INTRODUCTION TO PHILATELY

CHAPTER I

THE COMING OF POSTAGE STAMPS

THE POSTMAN'S KNOCK, or ring, is the most familiar and welcome of sounds. There are few homes where it is not heard at least once a day. A hundred years ago the postman was a rare visitor, and not always a welcome one. He brought then, as now, good or bad news, but the postage rates were high, and they had to be paid to the postman on delivery of the letter. Generally it was not just a matter of a few pence. A single sheet of letter from London to Edinburgh cost 1s. 1½d. in 1839; if there were two sheets, it cost double, and if the packet weighed an ounce, it was charged as four single letters. Thus the postman in Edinburgh would demand 4s. 6d. for delivering a letter which today can cost only 4d., paid in advance by the convenient means of a postage stamp.

Rowland Hill and a band of active reformers in the early years of the Victorian era, however, were able to show ways and means of giving the public an efficient and cheap service of correspondence throughout the country, without detriment to the public revenue. The coming of the railways, the extension of education, and the spread of newspapers and periodicals all helped to drive home the arguments of the postal reformers that a well-ordered postal administration could profitably convey letters to all parts of the Kingdom at a uniform rate of postage of a penny per half-ounce letter, paid in advance. Prepayment was an essential part of the plan: the postage stamp provided the ideal solution of a simple means by which the people of town and country could prepay their letters.

Parliament passed the Uniform Penny Postage Act in

1839. The uniform penny rate came into force on January 10th, 1840, but it had to be prepaid in cash, for no kind of stamp was yet ready for sale to the public. Rowland Hill rather favoured the use of stamped envelopes or wrappers. William Mulready was commissioned to prepare a design for these. A combination of artists and engravers was working at the same time upon the adhesive labels bearing the simple device of the Queen's head.

The public first saw the " covers " and the " labels " on May 1st, 1840, although they were not to be used until May 6th.

Mulready's elaborate and imaginative design, although it had the commendation of the Academicians, did not appeal to the people. The artist pictured Britannia sending out winged messengers to the four points of the compass, a

Mulready's design for the letter-sheets and envelopes, 1840. It presents the first instance of a philatelic " error "; the angel at top right has only one leg.

prophetic suggestion we can now appreciate better than people living in the first half of the nineteenth century.

In 1840 the design was lampooned in the Press and scorned by the public, who much preferred the little label stamps with the " glutinous wash " on their backs, the sheet margins of which advised : " In wetting the Back be careful not to remove the Cement."

The majority of stamp collectors confine their collections to postage stamps of the adhesive class, of which the One Penny Black and the Two Pence Blue issued by Great Britain in 1840 were the first.[1] Finely engraved so that they might not be easily counterfeited, they were simple and dignified, and in inscription went direct to their purpose : " Postage One Penny " or " Postage Two Pence." It was unnecessary, with the young Queen's head upon them, that they should bear the name of the country, and to this day the Sovereign's head upon our stamps suffices to denote their origin in the Mother Country.

The success of uniform penny postage was made clear in the results beyond the expectations of the reformers. In place of 76 million letters on which postage was paid in 1839, there were 169 million in 1840, and within five years this figure was nearly doubled.

· · · · ·

The postal reform in Great Britain was noted with interest abroad. The great nations of the Continent and America had problems not identical with our own in creating a uniform rate of postage, and they were slow to adopt the principle of prepayment by means of postage stamps or stamped stationery. Their peoples had long been habituated to sending their letters, etc., at the expense of those who received them. There was a general idea that if the postage were paid in advance, it prejudiced the chance of delivery, whereas unpaid letters were secured by the fact

Plate 1, illustrations 1 and 2.

that the Post Office would see that it got the money. Another not uncommon notion was that it was little short of an insult to prepay the postage.

The Swiss Cantons, before the Confederation, were among the earliest followers of Great Britain in issuing adhesive stamps for prepayment. Zürich stamps came first, in March 1843, and Geneva produced its curiosity, a divisible stamp, in October of the same year. For the first large country to have stamps we turn to far-off Brazil, which issued the so-called "Bull's-eye" stamps on August 1st, 1843 (Plate 1).

The year 1844 witnessed no additions to the slender list but in 1845 the canton of Basle issued its " dove " stamp, and the Postmaster of New York produced a fine stamp of his own. The first British Colony to issue stamps was Mauritius, 1847, and the first Government postage stamps of the United States came in the same year. With Bermuda in 1848, Bavaria, Belgium, and France in 1849, the first ten years of postage stamps shows but ten countries following Britain's lead.

Then the use of stamps became widespread. In the next fifteen years most of the principal States of Europe and America, and many British possessions overseas, had joined in. In 1874 the General Postal Union was started, and a year later became the Universal Postal Union, to which the postal administrations throughout the world belong. Its rulings regulate the interchange of mails and services between all countries, and one of its essential requirements is that its members use the system of prepayment by stamps.

.   .   .   .   .

The foregoing chronology of stamp issuing will make it clear that for the first ten years there were few stamps of different kinds to stimulate the collecting instinct. There were people even then who were watching the slow spread of the stamp system, especially among those who had taken some part in the campaign for postal reform. In the second decade of the postage stamp era the number of countries issuing stamps increased more rapidly, and various changes had been made in the stamps of the countries that started earlier.

In the middle 'fifties there were collectors quietly gathering the different examples of stamps they could find, but probably without any special aim or purpose. By 1861 there were many more stamps, and more people collecting them, for the most part individually and independently. Very few of them were in touch with or knew of the existence of other collectors.

Just before Christmas 1861 a little booklet was published in Paris entitled *Catalogue des Timbres-Poste créés dans les divers Etats du Globe*. It was the first published catalogue of postage stamps. It is remarkable that at that date the compiler, Alfred Potiquet, was able to list no fewer than 1,080 adhesive postage stamps and 132 stamped envelopes. Still more wonderful the total seems when he tells us " the majority are in our collection, and we have seen most of the others. Our work is thus exact, but we do not doubt it is incomplete." A second edition appeared in March 1862, giving 1,253 items, but by this time there were rival catalogues from Paris and Brussels, and an English boy, Frederick Booty, compiled one under the title *Aids to Stamp Collectors*, which was published at Brighton in April 1862. Two other English catalogues made their first appearance in the same year, which also witnessed the earliest publications of the kind in Germany and the United States.

It was thus in 1862 that the collecting of postage stamps first became a popular and widespread hobby, not only in Britain, but abroad. Journals and magazines devoted to the new hobby sprang up, and some of the early ones are usefully consulted to this day.

From a glance at the early English catalogues we get a notion of how the number of stamps was growing. The first edition of Mount Brown's catalogue, in May 1862, listed 1,200 stamps, but this figure had doubled by the fifth edition in March 1864. One hundred and twenty thousand varieties would be an under-estimate of the number of all classes of stamps on Mount Brown's system today.

The nominal aim of the early collector was to gather together a complete collection of every known variety of postage stamp. Most likely none ever achieved it, nor has anyone since. Completeness is as illusive as the horizon, to which it is better to travel hopefully than to arrive.

The magnificent collection in the British Museum, bequeathed to the nation by the late Thomas Keay Tapling, M.P., who died in 1891, is, however, nearly complete in all issues, foreign as well as British, from 1840 to 1890. It is a great asset for philatelic students to be able to acquire a good knowledge of the rarer stamps by studying them here, in cases specially devised to enable visitors to inspect the 4,752 album pages without risk to the stamps.

CHAPTER II

THE COLLECTOR'S ACCESSORIES

STAMP COLLECTING OWES PART of its popularity to the ease with which one can start a collection. Anyone can start. In earlier days all that was necessary was a few stamps, an exercise book, and a pot of paste or gum.

The modern collector would not be content with such a start, and would know from the outset that paste or glue is taboo in the collector's outfit. An exercise book is still useful in default of an album, but albums specially prepared for stamps need not be expensive; there is a large variety of all grades to meet every requirement.

Apart from stamps, the modern collector's chief accessories are a few simple articles designed to keep the collection in order, to preserve the specimens from damage or loss, and to assist in studying and classifying. A beginner may count himself well set up for a good start with an album, catalogue, tweezers, magnifying-glass, stamp hinges and a perforation gauge.

The Album.—On the same principle that a small family would be lost in a large house, the beginner, even if he can afford a big, elaborate album, should content himself with one of modest capacity to carry him through the early stages of his collecting. Bear in mind that your chief need all along will be stamps, and more stamps. The money spent on a large and luxurious album for a beginner would be better expended on stamps. Nothing is more disheartening to a young collector than to discover after he has got his first few hundreds of different stamps that the pages of his big album look as bare and empty as they were when he began. A small collection is lost in the big album.

You will want to turn to your stamps without having to hunt through lots of blank pages. You will want to show others your collection, and the more compact it is the better they will appreciate it.

The printed and fast-bound stamp album is almost a thing of the past. It was either too big or too small. There was no elasticity about it. The collector of today has come over to the practical advantages of the loose-leaf album. The great collector uses loose-leaf albums exclusively, and having selected the style he prefers, he adds album after album as required.

To the beginner the loose-leaf album offers a means of keeping his collection compact, adding page by page as he has need of it. So let your first album be a loose-leaf one. Choose it for a nice quality of paper, with a surface that will not peel off, leaving an ugly space, when a stamp is moved. The pages will be ruled in feint quadrillé pattern to help you arrange the stamps symmetrically. Avoid album leaves that are printed with heavy borders or distracting ornamentation. And lastly, look to the " fitting " of the binder—the simpler it is the better. There are many patent gadgets for such binders, and the more complex they are, the more liable to get out of order. The simplest form of binders are the spring-backs, which are excellent if you keep them tidily and do not put too many leaves in a single cover. Other useful, and rather more expensive, fittings have pegs or bolts holding the album leaves in position.

The Catalogue.—I have placed this second in my list of accessories, for without one the collector might as well be working in the dark. The catalogue is an illustrated and priced list of the different postage stamps issued by the countries of the world. It is generally a dealer's price list, but, quite apart from the price quotations for the stamps, it is the chief and handiest guide to what postage stamps exist. The illustrations help us to identify our stamps, and to get them into a rational chronological order.

The leading catalogues are revised frequently, and it is a false economy to work with an out-of-date edition. The revision is necessary, not only because the dealer's prices are subject to variation, but because there is a considerable crop of " new issues " of stamps to be added to the catalogues each year.

The beginner will be best advised to use a simple form of catalogue. Stanley Gibbons' *Simplified Catalogue* is excellent, and is sold by stamp dealers and booksellers.

Messrs. Stanley Gibbons, Ltd., issue a much larger catalogue, going more deeply into the minor varieties of stamps; it is on this that the advanced collector works, and its price quotations form a basis for world-wide transactions in the stamp market. It appears in three volumes: British Commonwealth; Europe and Colonies; America, Asia and Africa.

In the United States, the leading catalogues are *Scott's Standard Postage Stamp Catalogue* and the *Gibbons-Whitman Postage Stamp Catalogue*. Similar works are issued by the prominent dealers in France, Germany, and Switzerland.

Tweezers.—A simple but important accessory which should always be at hand. Get them preferably from a stamp dealer, and in any case do not use sharp-pointed tweezers, which may prick holes in your stamps. The important thing about tweezers is to use them, and not touch stamps with the fingers more than you can help. It comes easy with a little practice to do all the operations of sorting and mounting with the tweezers; in fact, easier than with the fingers.

Magnifying-glass.—You probably have a suitable one about the house. You do not need a high magnification, and in using the glass it is worth your while to cultivate the habit of *not* closing the other eye. Most people screw up one eye and close the other when using a glass, and that is not good for the eyes.

Stamp Hinges.—Many good stamps in olden times were ruined by being stuck fast in albums. The paste or glue disintegrated them, or they got torn by later owners in trying to remove them from old albums. Modern philately owes much to the inventor (whoever he was) of the stamp hinge. Specially prepared stamp hinges are so cheap that there is no excuse for using makeshift hinges from " stamp-edging " or gummed music rolls, either of which may result in damage to stamps.

The proper stamp hinges are quite thin, coated on one side with a pure, tasteless gum, and are so made that they will peel off the album page or off the stamp without leaving an unsightly mark on the page or spoiling the stamp.

The use of these hinges is simple; like most simple things, it requires care and attention. Laying the stamp face downwards, take the little gum strip with the tweezers and fold it to form the hinge, just touch the shorter arm of the hinge with the tongue and lightly press it in position at the top of the back of the stamp. Then moisten (ever so lightly) the longer arm and place stamp and hinge in the proper space on the album page.

Normally, stamps are hinged at the top, quite close to the perforations, so that any stamp may be turned over on its back without taking it out of the album. Nowadays many stamps are issued in large sizes, and my practice with these is to fold my hinge the long way, and to apply it to the longer dimension of the stamp. Thus if the longer dimension be horizontal, affix the hinge at the top back. If the vertical dimension be the longer, the hinge is applied to the right-hand side of the back of the stamp; when the stamp is in position in the album, the hinge is at the left, and folds or opens the same way as the album does, thus minimising risk of creasing the stamp.

Perforation Gauge.—As we shall see later on, many stamps alike in design and colour differ in the style or measure of their perforations. It is important we should be able to distinguish differences in the perforation, and this need present no difficulty to the beginner who is provided with a perforation gauge.

The mechanical perforation of paper to render separation easy was almost unknown when the first postage stamps were issued in 1840. The first perforated stamps were issued in Great Britain in 1854, and the process of perforation for a considerable time presented such mechanical difficulties that the system only spread slowly to the stamps of other countries.

Thus the perforation of stamps was a British invention, but French philatelists were the first to measure the different gauges. Dr. J. A. Legrand, who devised the method of measurement, and invented the perforation gauge, being a Frenchman, took the metrical system as his basis, and measured the number of perforated holes punched in a given space of 2 centimetres.

You could take a metrical rule and count them, but this would be slow and tedious. The gauge is a neat card showing a graded scale of the chief stamp perforations in 2-centimetre sections. By sliding the perforated edge of a stamp along this scale, you find a set of dots coincides with the stamp perforations. The number at the scale gives you the gauge of the perforation. Thus the figure 12 denotes there are 12 punched holes to the 2 centimetres, or the figure $13\frac{1}{2}$ means that there are $13\frac{1}{2}$ holes. In the former case we describe it as Perf(orated) 12, and in the latter Perf. $13\frac{1}{2}$.

Often a stamp has a different gauge of perforation in

the horizontal direction from that of the vertical sides. This is called a compound perforation. The expression Perf. 15 × 14 means that the horizontal (top and bottom) perforation gauges 15 and the sides 14.

In giving perforation measures, the horizontal is given first. In rare cases where all four edges give different measures they are named in the order of the clock, " top, right, bottom, left," and would be expressed as " Perf. 12 × 11 × 13 × 14." In practice it is rarely necessary to measure more than one, or at most two edges.

With the perforation gauge (which is in universal use) measuring perforations is easy and speedy. Just dismiss from your mind any idea of counting the perforations of the stamp itself. The edges of a stamp may be shorter or longer than 2 centimetres, but where they fit on the scale they can be taken to denote how many punches there were in a measured length of 2 centimetres, which gives you the correct " Perf."

It is not necessary to measure the perforations of all your stamps. The catalogue tells you what the perf. is in most cases; sometimes there are stamps alike in appearance but with different perforations, and these you will measure to know which yours are. Likewise, if you have any suspicion that a stamp is a reprint or a forgery, one of the first things to do is to compare your stamp with the gauge of perforation as given in the catalogue.

There will be other small accessories you will find useful additions to your outfit as you go along. There are books of various sizes furnished with transparent slots or shelves for arranging and keeping stamps before you are ready to mount them in your album. Small slim booklets or pocket cases similarly provided with slots enable you to carry stamps about.

If watermarks prove difficult to see, a benzine cup or

" watermark detector" will help you. It is only a black-bottomed tray, or a small porcelain slab will do. The stamp is laid face downwards on the black surface, and a little benzine dropped on the back will reveal the watermark device for a moment or two before the benzine evaporates. Very few old stamps suffer harm in benzine, but modern photogravure stamps are liable to lose their colour.

Peroxide of hydrogen in solution as commonly sold by chemists is useful for restoring the colours of stamps that have got blackened through exposure (see De-sulphurate in Chapter XIX). Old line-engraved stamps like the 1d. red and 2d. blue Great Britain may be immersed in peroxide, but where more delicate colours or only parts of stamps have been discoloured, the peroxide should be applied with a camel-hair brush to the parts affected.

If stamps that have been left about in a dry atmosphere curl themselves up, you will probably damage them by trying to flatten them out. They will uncurl naturally if you place them in a tight-fitting box along with a small moist sponge, keeping the sponge well away from the stamps. A cigar box or flat cigarette tin will do. Do not leave the stamps to absorb more moisture than is necessary to enable them to uncurl; after allowing them to dry, keep them flat.

When stamps get stuck back-to-back or face-to-back, do not attempt to pull them apart. Take a flat cork and let it float in a small basin of hot water, with the stamps on its dry top; the steam will soon loosen them sufficiently to pull them apart without damage. This is also a convenient way of removing paper off the backs of stamps where there is any risk of colours being soluble in water.

While there are many stamps that can be quite safely immersed in water, it is safer for the young collector to float them instead of soaking them. Not attempting to do

CHAPTER III

STARTING A COLLECTION

IT IS EASIER TO get together a large collection of stamps today than it has ever been. In the early days of this century, the average schoolboy collection rarely contained over a thousand varieties, slowly acquired from current correspondence, some swapping at school, and occasional purchases from " approval sheets."

Today it is possible for any young collector to start—numerically—where his prototype of fifty years ago left off. While the older stamps are steadily becoming scarcer, there are so many more varieties of the commoner stamps available.

The common stamps are normally the basis of any collection. Stamp collecting as a hobby does not depend for its main and wide interest on rarity. The beginner gains his early knowledge of stamps from the kinds that come most readily to his possession. He should not worry about the stamps that are beyond his reach. In forming a representative general collection, either of the stamps of the whole world, or of the entire British Commonwealth, the collector is learning the game. The stamps he acquires introduce him to the intricacies of variation in design, colour, paper, watermark, and perforation. He is going through a helpful and interesting kind of apprenticeship to philately, and everything he learns from the common stamps will be useful in later and advanced stages of collecting.

A fairly small expenditure will give the modern beginner 1,000 different postage stamps to start with. Certainly they will be common stamps, but they will be clean, and after providing some interesting evenings in sorting and identifying them, they will be ready for putting into the album.

If funds permit of a bigger start, it is an economy to buy a larger variety packet. The first 1,000 are cheap, but every additional 500 or 1,000 varieties beyond the first cost more on account of the relatively greater difficulty of getting them.

Over the first 1,000, sold by the dealers loose and unsorted, the larger packet collections are usually sold mounted in booklets, the stamps being arranged in countries. Thus the preliminary sorting is not required. You can transfer them by degrees into your album, country by country.

If you wish only to collect the stamps of the British Commonwealth, variety packets work out more expensive. Should you intend from the start to collect these stamps only, you will do well to purchase a packet of this kind. As one who has roamed the whole wide world of stamps, and derived endless pleasure from foreign as well as British Colonial stamps, I commend you to start collecting stamps from all countries. Let your collecting interests survey the world from China to Peru, until later on, when you have gained a wide general knowledge of stamps, you may select for yourself the country or countries that attract you most. Do not imagine that either the time or the money spent on starting on the world-wide plan will be wasted. You will be equipped with an extensive knowledge that will always prove helpful.

·   ·   ·   ·   ·

Assuming that our beginner has obtained his start in the form of a variety packet, and infused life into his album by putting the stamps into it, whence are the additions to come to carry on the collection? Lucky is the collector who has access to the discarded envelopes from the correspondence of a relative or a firm whose transactions are large, colonial or international. Many useful additions may come that way or by gift.

The modern stamp collector will not get very far in extending his collection by stamps derived from either the waste-paper basket or by gift. Rarely is a worth-while collection obtained without expenditure. Gifts may fill up gaps here and there, but few would be satisfied without some more systematic way of developing a collection.

The main source of our supplies of stamps will be the stamp trade. Once your collection is well started, you will find the windows (and interiors) of the stamp shops full of interest and alluring offers of stamps, a large proportion of which would make welcome additions to your collection. The collector will occasionally get bargains even from the biggest stamp shops, but do not depend on " bargains." You will have your share of lucky purchases as your knowledge of stamps grows, but stamps offered at " bargain " prices are not always such bargains as they appear. Be prepared to pay fair and reasonable prices for your stamps, and preferably deal with stamp firms of reputation.

Collectors are not all conveniently situated to visit the dealers' establishments, and most of us have to transact at least part of our business with them by post. In the early stages of collecting, the system of the approval sheets operates usefully. These are small selections of stamps mounted and priced on sheets, from which the customer can make his selection, returning the sheet with remittance for the stamps kept.

For the collector who has started with a moderate-size packet of " all different," the principal dealers offer a convenient and inexpensive way of strengthening the nucleus collection by " long sets." A long set consists of all different stamps of one country. A few stamps in such sets will duplicate some already in his album, but it will prove an economy to buy the long set, and the duplicates will come in handy. Dealers also advertise special offers in the philatelic journals.

An important source of stamps for collectors is the auction room. Stamp auctions are conducted by experts, who devote their businesses almost exclusively to the sale of stamps by auction or private treaty. Much of their work consists in selling important collections, broken up into suitable lots. Detailed and well-illustrated catalogues are widely circulated, and many of the bids come from country and overseas buyers by post, cable, and radio.

Lots at a stamp auction may consist of a single rare stamp or a considerable collection, and many philatelists find the auction sales the most helpful and fascinating means of improving their collections. It is often possible for a comparative beginner to buy a ready-made collection at an auction and treat it as the nucleus from which he can build up a much bigger and better collection. The auctions also afford opportunities for strengthening your collection country by country.

New issues of postage stamps continue to appear from all over the world, and collectors like to get them as soon as they can. Some of the leading dealers conduct special New Issue Services. By importing all new stamps in quantity, they are able to supply subscribers with the stamps as soon as they reach this country. A small charge is made over the face value of the stamps for this useful service, which helps to keep the collection up to date. Such services are graded to suit subscribers' purses.

Most collectors do a certain amount of exchanging with other collectors. Whatever your sources of supply, you will find you acquire duplicates. If you meet other collectors, you may swap your duplicates for stamps you want. If you belong to a stamp club, your opportunities of exchanging with other members will be increased. A system of " exchange packets " is operated by many philatelic societies and exchange clubs.

The method of the exchange packet is simple, if somewhat slow. The club superintendent provides sheets of uniform size. On these members mount stamps they seek to dispose of, marking the price asked, and send the sheets to the superintendent. The latter puts the sheets received into a packet, which is then circulated to each in turn. Members can thus select stamps from each other's sheets, sign, and enter the amounts taken; when the circuit is complete, the officer breaks up the packet, sending back unsold stamps, and giving an account of each member's sales and purchases, which can then be balanced in cash.

A question that has been put to me many times is, " Should I collect unused or used stamps? " You may in time develop a preference for one or the other, but there is no need to restrict the growth of your collection by an arbitrary choice. Some stamps are more accessible unused than used, but the majority are cheaper used. It requires rather keener judgment to select fine used copies than fine unused. The question has little point in it nowadays; it is a hangover from olden days when young collectors viewed all or nearly all unused stamps with suspicion.

CHAPTER IV

ARRANGEMENT AND WRITING-UP

A STAMP COLLECTION IS a thing of gradual growth, and it is a great advantage if it can be preserved in an album that grows with the collection. As explained in Chapter II, the loose-leaf albums have so many advantages over the fast-bound books, that they are now in almost universal use among philatelists.

On a blank page you follow your own notions of arrangement and symmetry; you record your own impressions, ideas, and knowledge as you go along. You supply the human touch that gives individuality and added charm to the collection.

Laying out the stamps on the album leaves should not present any difficulty. The leaves, although nominally blank, have a feint ground of one-eighth-inch squares, with feint guide-marks showing the true centre of the mounting area, and also the middle at top, bottom and sides. With these convenient guides you may set out your stamps in regular rows, but you can do better than that.

As a general principle, you will start a fresh page for each country. The stamps of any one country fall into groups, sets, or issues; these are best placed in their chronologica order, starting a new row for each issue.

A set or issue of seven values could be mounted thus:

$$1 \quad 2 \quad 3 \quad 4 \quad 5 \quad 6$$
$$7$$

but as two rows are required for it the seven stamps would be better displayed in one of the following ways:

$$1 \quad 2 \quad 3 \qquad 1 \quad 2 \quad 3 \quad 4 \qquad 1 \quad 2$$
$$4 \quad 5 \quad 6 \quad 7 \qquad 5 \quad 6 \quad 7 \qquad 3 \quad 4 \quad 5 \quad 6 \quad 7$$

The quadrillé ground on the album page makes it a very simple matter to adopt these and other varied forms of display. Let us follow, for example, the first of these displayed forms.

Starting not too close to the top of the page, find the centre and mount stamp 2. It should be parallel with the horizontal lines of the quadrillé ruling. Now allow two, three, or four squares to left and right, mounting stamps 1 and 3.

The second row should come not less than four squares below the stamps in the first row. Instead of an odd number, we have now an even number of stamps. The centre beneath stamp 2 will be a blank interval the same width as you have allowed between the stamps on the top row, say four squares wide. Work from the centre outwards, thus—stamp 5, another interval of four squares, and then stamp 4; 6 and 7 have then to be similarly spaced to the right. Between one full set and the next a little more space may be allowed, say, six squares down instead of four. Here perhaps our set consists of eleven stamps, which may be set out as:

$$1 \quad 2 \quad 3 \quad 4 \quad 5$$
$$6 \quad 7 \quad 8 \quad 9 \quad 10 \quad 11$$

or, as the high value may be a stamp of abnormal size:

$$1 \quad 2 \quad 3$$
$$4 \quad 5 \quad 6 \quad 7$$
$$8 \quad 9 \quad 10$$
$$11$$

These are only suggestions, and are capable of almost infinite variation. Before passing on to consider the arrangement of advanced or specialised collections, a few of the problems of the beginner call for attention.

Optimism is a strong point with the beginner, his enthusiasm is keen, his ambition expansive. Arranging his first loose-leaf album with the aid of his catalogue, he is confronted with the problem of what spaces to leave for stamps he has yet to acquire.

Here common sense will serve better than overweening ambition. If the earliest stamp you have of Mauritius is the 1 cent purple and ultramarine of 1895, it is wasteful of energy and album leaves to mark up spaces for the historic but almost unattainable issues of 1847 to 1859.

Where there is good reason to hope you will get the stamps in due course, provision may be made for adding them without remounting those already in your album, but you want your collection, even now, to have the appearance of being a collection of stamps, and not of empty spaces which are neither interesting nor heartening.

Your collection should show clearly and as compactly as is consistent with not overcrowding what stamps you have; no need to emphasise unduly the stamps you do not possess.

SPECIALISTS

For the advanced collector or specialist the loose-leaf album has long been indispensable. No lay-out in a printed album can provide adequately for the multifarious and varied items that come within the scope of the specialised collection, so the unfettered freedom of the loose-leaf album with its pages of quadrillé guiding squares is a necessity to the specialist.

The laying-out of the ordinary stamps in well-marked groups applies to the specialist's collection, but he will still more particularly avoid crowding his pages. The displayed groups may no longer be sets or issues, but groups of the same stamp in a sequence of shades or other varieties. He will have to accommodate pairs and strips and blocks of stamps. Some collectors who have no difficulty in setting out straightforward rows of single stamps make a poor show when it comes to fitting in a block or strip; most of them would avoid this difficulty if they did not attempt to put too much on their pages. It is no false economy to allow a whole row for a strip or half a page to a block if you cannot otherwise make an appropriate and symmetrical lay-out without crowding the page. Similarly, a stamp on the original letter or envelope, or a portion of it, may well be given a half or even a whole page to itself.

WRITING-UP

Up to the present we have not discussed what should be written or drawn upon the album pages. Our stamps are neatly set out on pages that bear no other print than the quadrillé ruling.

The beginner will be wise to avoid too much writing-up. Concise notes are to be preferred to long descriptions. The name of the country may be inscribed at the top of each page, or you may prefer to use the plainly printed gummed labels, as supplied by most stamp dealers, with the names of stamp-issuing countries.

In the simplest form of writing-up, only the date of issue and the title (if any) of the issue are necessary. The writing should be plain; avoid fanciful writing. If your ordinary calligraphy is not too clear, a neat form of printed lettering may be used, not too large, and yet not so small as to make reading difficult.

An example of the simplest form of writing-up is:

UNITED STATES

1893.—Fourth Centenary of the Discovery of America.

For countries where importance attaches to watermarks and perforations, the following is the simplest form, showing name of country, date, watermark, perforation, as, for example:

MALTA

1903.—Wmk. Crown C.A. Perf. 14.

These are simple forms of writing-up, though any points that appear to the collector to possess special interest may be the subject of additional notes which may make the collection more attractive to friends, but avoid stating the obvious. If a blue stamp is plainly marked 2½d., there is no need to write " 2½d. blue " to describe what is plain to all. Similarly, if a stamp is a three-cornered one, it serves no reasonable purpose to write " Triangular " above or below it.

A small arrow or pointed mark will call attention to some curious mark, flaw, or error on the stamp, but such indications should be used with moderation.

Writing-up should be done with pen and ink, using the pen and nib that suit you best or a mapping pen for neat, printed lettering. Ordinary blue-black writing ink or Indian ink should be used; avoid aniline violet inks. If you make pencil notes or marks on the pages, take care never to use an indelible pencil.

It is not within the scope of this chapter to enlarge upon the writing-up of specialised collections by advanced collectors. It may, however, be useful to set out in their proper sequence the several details which it is desirable (where applicable and known) to state in order to present a concise philatelic history of a stamp or issue:

Date of issue, design, artist, engraver, printer, mode of production, paper, including watermarks, perforation, date of supersession, quantity printed and issued.

THE SPECIMEN PAGES (Plate 3)

AUSTRIA.—A page of pictorial stamps of varying sizes.

In the second set it is not altogether necessary to write in the names of the towns, as they are indicated upon the stamps, but not very prominently.

BULGARIA.—This page shows a lay-out allowing spaces for addition of stamps yet to be obtained. The short, horizontal pencil lines show where the other stamps should come, but in practice it is not necessary to indicate the spaces with lines; a dot at each extremity of the positions would serve equally well.

CHAPTER V

STAMPS THAT PUZZLE BEGINNERS

THERE WAS NO NAME of the issuing country on the first adhesive postage stamps, just the Queen's head, the word " Postage," and the value in English words. A century has elapsed, and still the stamps of Great Britain pass nameless in the international mails: the familiar effigy of the Sovereign renders the name of the Mother Country unnecessary.

In the summer of 1843, Brazil followed the British procedure for her first stamps, except in the matter of the Emperor's portrait. For over twenty years, 1843–66, the Brazilian stamps bore numerals; no name, not even a word to denote the currency or the purpose of the stamps. Collectors are familiar with them, and know them as 1843 " large figures " (nicknamed *ohlos de boi*, or Bull's-eyes), 1844 " slanting figures " (Goat's-eyes) and " upright figures " for the issues of 1850 and 1861. With the coming of the Emperor's head issue of 1866, the name " Brazil " appeared on the stamps, changed in modern times to " Brasil."

One British colony issued a 2*d.* stamp in 1852, locally engraved, and lacking the colony's name. The Melbourne artist, in presenting Queen Victoria in her regal robes and seated in the Coronation Chair, may have deemed the colony's name Victoria to be superfluous (Plate 9, Stamp 11).

The majority of stamps bear the name of the issuing country in words and characters familiar to us all. In some cases they are spelt differently from the English renderings; in others where the name is lacking some distinguishing word or emblem will be readily identified from the alphabetical lists given in this chapter. Where countries have used Slavonic or Greek alphabets, a short supplementary list is given in those alphabets which should make identification of the country of origin a very simple task.

In the case of the Oriental countries it will be useful to memorise a few distinguishing emblems :

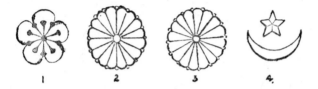

Cherry Blossom.—The five-leaf cherry blossom is the emblem of Korea. Sometimes mistaken for a plum blossom (Fig. 1).

Chrysanthemum.—A sixteen-petalled chrysanthemum up to May 1947 appeared on every stamp issue of Japan except the first. Any Japanese stamp with other than sixteen petals in the chrysanthemum is a forgery (Figs. 2 and 3).

Crescent, with five-pointed star. Symbol found on stamps of several Mohammedan countries, but chiefly on Turkish stamps (Fig. 4).

Four Crowns, set to form a cross. This is the emblem of Mongolia (known as the *Otshira*); it appears with value in cents, or 1 dollar, on the first issue, 1924 (Fig 5).

Hammer and Sickle.—Emblem of the Union of Soviet Socialist Republics, met with on stamps of Soviet Russia and associated Soviet Republics: Armenia, Azerbaijan, Georgia, Trans-Caucasia (Fig. 6).

Orchid.—Emblem of Manchuria. Values in fen (fn.) or yuan (yn.) (Fig. 7).

Tughra.—An elaborate emblem of authority in Mohammedan countries, used as Britain uses a royal cypher or monogram. A tughra sometimes presents the most ready means of identifying stamps of Turkey, Hejaz-Nejd (Saudi Arabia), Thessaly (octagonal stamps) (Fig. 8).

9   10.   11.

Trident.—A variety of trident overprints on Russian stamps denote their circulation in the Ukraine, 1918. The device is included in the Ukraine stamp designs of 1918 and 1919 (Figs. 9 and 10).

Wheel of Eternity.—Emblem on first issue of the Tannou Touva Republic, North Mongolia, 1926 (Fig. 11).

12.   13.   14.

Yin-yang.—An Oriental symbol of the two principles of life, male and female in animate things, and light and darkness. It is represented in varying but easily recognised forms in stamp designs of Korea, Mongolia, and as a watermark device in stamps of China (Figs. 12 and 13).

Z.—Cypher of the Armenian Posts, overprinted on Russian stamps used in Armenia in 1920 (Fig. 14).

IDENTIFICATION BY INSCRIPTION

The index words or initials in this list are prominent in the stamp inscriptions, and are clues for quick identification; the keys are not necessarily translations. Overprints or surcharges are listed in italics; designs in small capitals.

A & T.—Annam and Tonquin.

Açores.—Azores.

Africa.—Portuguese Africa.

A.O. — Afrika Oost. — Ruanda-Urundi.

A payer—te betalen.—Belgium, postage due.

A percevoir.—Belgium, France, French Colonies, Monaco, postage due.

ARABESQUES.—Egypt; Hejaz-Nejd, now Saudi Arabia.

Avisporto.—Denmark, newspaper stamp.

B. on Straits Settlements.—Bangkok.

BATYM.—Batum.

Bayer., Bayern.—Bavaria.

B.C.A.—British Central Africa, now Malawi.

Belgie, Belgique.—Belgium; German occupation: Belgien.

Braunschweig.—Brunswick.

C.C.C.P.—Soviet Russia.

C.E.F. — China Expeditionary Force; Cameroons Expeditionary Force.

C. CH.—Cochin China.

Cesko-Slovenska.—Czecho-slovakia.

Chiffre Taxe.—France, postage due.

CHRYSANTHEMUM.—Japan—see Symbols, Figs. 2 and 3.

Comunicaciones.—Spain.

Confed. Granadina. — Granada Confederation (Colombia).

Continente.—Portugal.

Correio.—Portugal, Brazil.

Correos.—Spain and Colonies; many Latin American countries.

Correspondencia urgente.—Spain, express.

Côte d' Ivoire.—Ivory Coast.

Côte Française des Somalis.— French Somali Coast.

CPBNJA.—Serbia.

CRESCENT. — Turkey — see Symbols, Fig. 4.

Cross Overprint.—Generally denotes a Red Cross stamp.

CROWN AND POSTHORN.—Hungary.

CROWNS (4) in cross-form.— Mongolia—see Symbols, Fig. 5.

Danmark.—Denmark.

Dansk-Vestindien.—Danish West Indies.

Deficit.—Peru, postage due.

Deutsch - Neu - Guinea.—German New Guinea.

Deutsch-Ostafrika.—German East Africa.

Deutschösterreich.—Austria.

Deutsch-Südwest-Afrika. — German South-West Africa.

Deutsches Reich.—German Empire (Germany).
Dienstmarke.—Germany, official.
Dienst-sache.—Württemberg, municipal service.
Diligencia.—Uruguay.
D.J.—Djibouti.
Drzava S.H.S.—Jugoslavia.

Eagle.—Bosnia.
E.E.F.—Egyptian Expeditionary Force (Palestine).
Eesti.—Estonia.
EE. UU. de C. E.S. del T.—Tolima (Colombia).
E.F.O.—French Oceanic Establishments.
Eire.—Ireland.
Elua Keneta.—Hawaii.
Emp. Franc.—France.
Emp. Ottoman.—Turkey, Eastern Roumelia.
Equateur—Ecuador.
Escuelas.—Venezuela.
Espana.—Spain.
Estensi.—Modena.
Estero.—Italian Levant offices.
Etablissements—de l' Inde,—de l' Oceanie.—French Indian, French Oceanic, Settlements.
Ethiopie, Etiopia.—Abyssinia (Ethiopia).

Falta de Porte.—Mexico bogus " postage dues."
Filipinas, Filipas., Filipnas.—Philippine Is.
Franc.—(Abbreviation) France.
Franco (i.e. free).—Switzerland.
Franco-bollo.—Italy, Roman States, Sardinia, Tuscany.
Franco Marke fünf (or sieben) Grote.—Bremen.

Franquicia postal.—Spain.
Freimarke.—Württemberg, Prussia.
Frimärke. — Denmark, Norway, Sweden.

G. on Cape of Good Hope.—Griqualand West.
G. & D.—Guadeloupe and Dependencies.
G.E.A.—Tanganyika.
Georgie.—Georgia.
Giuba.—Jubaland.
G.P.E.—Guadeloupe.
G.R.I.—New Britain; Samoa.
Grand Liban.—Great Lebanon.
Greek inscriptions (see page 35).
Guyane.—French Guiana.

Haute-Volta.—Upper Volta.
Helvetia.—Switzerland.
H.H. NAWAB SHAH BEGAM.—Bhopal.
Hrvatska.—Jugoslavia.
H.R.Z.G.L.—Holstein.

I.E.F.—Indian Expeditionary Force.
I.E.F. " D ".—Mosul (Iraq).
Impuesto de guerra.—Spain, war tax.
Inde. — French Indian Settlements.
India Port.—Portuguese India.
Inland.—Liberia.
Instruccion.—Venezuela.
Island.—Iceland.
Jubilé de l'union postale.—Switzerland (1900).
Kamerun.—Cameroons (German).
Kärnten.—Carinthia.
K.G.C.A.—Carinthia.

K.G.L. Post Frm.—Denmark, Danish West Indies.
K.K. Post-stempel. — Austria, Austrian-Italy.
Kais Königl. Post.—Austria.
KPHTH.—Crete.
Kr., Kreuzer.—Austria.
Kraljevstvo Srba, Hrvata, i Slovenaca.—Jugoslavia. (Kingdom of the Serbs, Croats, and Slovenes).
K. u. K. Feld Post.—Austria.
K. u. K. Militär Post.—Bosnia.
K. Württ.—Württemberg.

La Georgie.—Georgia.
Land-Post.—Baden.
Lattaquie.—Latakia.
Latvija.—Latvia.
Liban, Libanaise.—Lebanon.
Lietuva, Lietuvos.—Lithuania.
LION.—Abyssinia; Iran (Persia).
Lösen.—Sweden, postage due.
Litwa, Litwy.—Lithuania (Central).
L. Mc. L.—Trinidad (local).

Magyar.—Hungary.
MAPKA.—Russia.
Maroc.—Morocco (Kingdom).
Marruecos.—Morocco (Spanish).
MERCURY.—Austria.
Mejico.—Mexico.
Militär Post.—Bosnia.
Modonesi.—Modena.
Montevideo.—Uruguay.
Moyen Congo.—Middle Congo.

Napoletana.—Naples.
N.C.E.—New Caledonia.
Nederland.—Holland.
Ned. Indie.—Dutch Indies.
N.F.—Nyasaland Field Force (Tanganyika).

Nieuwe Republiek.—New Republic.
Norddeutscher Postbezirk.—North German Confederation.
Norge.—Norway.
Nouvelle Caledonie.—New Caledonia.
N.S.B.—Nossi Bé.
N.S.W.—New South Wales.
N.W. Pacific Islands.—North-West Pacific Islands.
N.Z.—New Zealand.

Oesterr, Oesterreich, or Österreich.—Austria.
Oltre Giuba.—Jubaland.
Orts Post.—Switzerland.
Oriental Emblems (see page 29).
Ottoman, Ottomanes.—Turkey.

P., P.G.S.—Perak.
Pacchi Postali.—Italy, parcel post.
Para.—Egypt, Serbia, Turkey, Levant.
Parm., Parmensi.—Parma.
P.C.C.P.—Russia.
P.E.—Egypt.
Pen.—Finland.
Piastre.—Egypt, Turkey, Palestine, Levant.
Pinsin.—Ireland (Eire).
Pohjois Inkeri.—Ingermanland.
POCCIA.—Russia.
Polska.—Poland.
Porte de Conducción.—**Peru.**
Porte franco.—Peru.
Porte de Mar.—Mexico.
Porteado.—Portugal and Colonies, postage due.
Porto.—Austria.
Porto piaster.—Austrian-Levant.
Postage, Postage and Revenue Postage Due.—Great Britain.

Post Stamp.—Hyderabad.
Postas le n'ioc.—Ireland (Eire), postage due.
Postat e Qeverries.—Albania.
Poste locale.—Switzerland.
Postes.—Alsace and Lorraine, Belgium, Luxembourg.
Postmarke.—Brunswick.
Postzegel.—Holland.
Preussen.—Prussia.
P.S.N.C.—Peru (Pacific Steam Navigation Co.).

Qeverries.—Albania.

R.—Jind.
Rayon.—Switzerland.
Recargo.—Spain.
Registered.—Liberia.
Reichspost.—Germany.
Republica Oriental.—Uruguay.
R.F.—France, and Colonies.
R.H.—Hayti.
Rialtar Sealadác na héireann.—Irish Provisional Government, now Ireland (Eire).
R.O.—Eastern Roumelia.
Romana, Romania.—Roumania.
Russian Inscriptions.—See Slavonic.

Sache.—Württemberg.
Sachsen.—Saxony.
Saorstát eireann.—Ireland (Eire).
Scrisorei.—Moldo-Wallachia (Roumania).
Segnatasse.—Italy, postage due.
S.H.—Schleswig-Holstein.
S.H.S.—Jugoslavia (Kingdom of the Serbs, Croats, and Slovenes).
Shqipenia, Shqiptare, etc.—Albania.
Slavonic characters (see page 35).

Sld. or soldi.—Austrian-Italy.
S.O.—Eastern Silesia.
Sobre porte.—Colombia, postage due.
S.P.M.—St. Pierre and Miquelon.
S.U.—Sungei Ujong.
Sultanat d'Anjouan.—Anjouan.
Suomi.—Finland.
Sverige.—Sweden.
S.W.A.—South West Africa.
Syrie, Syrienne.—Syria.

TAKCA.—Bulgaria, postage due.
Tassa Gazzette.—Modena.
Te betalen port.—Holland and Colonies, postage due. See also " a payer " above.
T.E.O.—Cilicia, Syria.
Tjeneste.—Denmark.
Toscano.—Tuscany.
Trident.—Ukraine. Symbols, Figs. 9 and 10.

U.A.R.—United Arab Republic, i.e. Egypt (values in m.) and Syria (values in p.).
U.G.—Uganda.
Uku Leta.—Hawaii.
Ultramar.—Spanish Colonies.
U.S.—United States.

Van Diemen's Land.—Tasmania.
Vom empfänger einzuziehen.—Danzig, postage due.

Württ.—Württemberg.

Y.C.C.P., Y.C.P.P.—Ukraine.
YKPAIHCbKA.—Ukraine.
Ykp. H. P.—West Ukraine.

Z.—Armenia. Symbols, Fig. 14.
Z.A.R.—(Transvaal).

Zeitungs.—Austria, Austrian-Italy.

Zuid West Africa.—South West Africa.

Inscriptions or overprints in Greek.

Crete.—ΚΡΗΤΗ.

Dedeagh.—ΔΕΔΕΑΓΑΤΣ.

Eastern Roumelia.—
ΑΝΑΤΟΛΙΚΗ ΡΩΜΥΛΙΑ.

Epirus.—ΗΠΕΙΡΟΣ.

Greece.—ΕΛΛ or ΕΛΛΑΣ.

Icaria.—ΙΚΑΡΙΑΣ.

Ionian Islands.—ΙΟΝΙΚΟΝ
ΚΡΑΤΟΣ

Lemnos.—ΛΗΜΝΟΣ.

Northern Epirus.—
Β. ΗΠΕΙΡΟΣ.

Samos.—ΣΑΜΟΥ.

Inscriptions or overprints in Slavonic.

Batum.—БАТУМ,
БАТУМСКАЯ.

Bulgaria.—БЪЛГАРИЯ or
БЪЛГАРСКА.

Montenegro.—ЦР. ГОРЕ,
ЦРНА ГОРА, or
ПОЩТЕЦРНЕГОРЕ.

Russia.—Early stamps can generally be recognised by the value, expressed in КОП (kopecks) or РУБ (roubles). Stamps in similar designs but with values in PEN (pennia) or MARKKAA (marks) are stamps of Finland; and another inscribed " ZA LOT KOP 10 " was issued for Poland. Since the Revolution Russian stamps have borne the name РОССІЯ, or the initials РССР., or СССР.

Serbia.—СРБИЈА or СРБСКА
or К. С. ПОЩТА.

Ukraine.—УКРАІНСЬКА

CHAPTER VI

USE YOUR EYES.
VARIETY THE SPICE OF PHILATELY

ONE OF THE SECRETS of success in stamp collecting rests in the proper use of the eyes. We do use them, but not all with a quick and intelligent observation of detail. Philately can help you to cultivate a ready perception of small differences in design, colour, and paper, and this eye-training is a useful asset in most departments of life.

It is not a question of microscopic detail, or the use of magnifying glasses. These may be necessary, but only rarely. The small, significant details which distinguish different stamps in a similar type or design are nearly always visible to the naked eye if the eye be accustomed to looking for them. A keen sense of colour differentiation is a help to advanced collectors, and it is as well to strive from the first to distinguish shades of the same colour.

For the beginner we shall give a number of examples of stamps that look alike, but are not. Before proceeding to do this, the importance of keen perception of details is to be stressed in safeguarding the collector from purchasing stamps with defects, e.g. a small tear; a pin-hole; a damaged stamp that has been more or less skilfully repaired; a cleaned stamp, from which a cancellation has been removed; a reprint; a fake; a forgery. The collector using his eyes intelligently and without strain develops a kind of extra sense in discerning the smallest variation from the normal. The same eye-training enables him to choose the best specimen from a page or more of copies in a dealer's stock book or approval selection.

In a long experience of stamp-collecting beginners, I

have been amazed at them discarding as duplicates such stamps as the Germania types of Germany of the issues of 1900 and 1902. The designs are similar, but the solitary inscription on the former reads "Reichpost," and on the second "Deutsches Reich."

More commonly will they pass over the United States small portrait stamps of 1890–93 and those of 1894–95. The former were the last U.S. post-age stamps printed by private contractors, and the 1894–95 was the first set printed by the Government Bureau of Engraving and Printing at 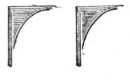 Washington. The Bureau took over the plates from the contractors, but in order to be able to distinguish their work they added the small triangular ornaments in the upper spandrels.

Only the unpractised eye of the beginner could miss the difference in the crowns of the small ¼ cent. de peseta stamps of Spain, 1872–77. One is a royal crown, and the other a mural (or republican)  crown, marking a notable phase in the long, troubled history of Spain.

The collector who has started with a packet of 500 or 1,000 " all different " is easily disposed to regard some of the stamps as being duplicates. It might happen that occasionally stamps are duplicated in such packets, but it is much more likely that the stamps are really different, although the difference may not be obvious. So before throwing out stamps that look as like as two peas, compare them carefully as to design, colour, paper, watermark, and perforation. Your catalogue will simplify the search for the elusive difference, as it tells you what varieties there are, and what to look for.

If you have started with a larger variety collection with the stamps already mounted in booklets, you are less likely to imagine the stamps are duplicated. You may still puzzle to find the differences, but this is all in the way of good practice in spotting varieties which will stand you in good stead later on.

Let us examine a few stamps of kinds that may be comprised in such packet collections.

The common 1*d.* lilac stamp of Queen Victoria's reign

exists in two distinct varieties. As first issued in July 1881 the stamp had fourteen dots or pearls in each of the four spandrels. The die was not quite satisfactory, so a new one was engraved, following the same design, but with the lettering clearer, and with sixteen dots or pearls in each spandrel. The earlier variety was in circulation for a few months; the later (sixteen-dot) was issued in December 1881, and continued in use for over twenty years. You may count the

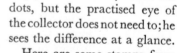

dots, but the practised eye of the collector does not need to; he sees the difference at a glance.

Here are some stamps from our packet that look much the same, and appear to be Russian. Some of them are, but those with the little circles rising like bubbles at each side of the oval were the stamps used in Finland under Russian domination.

Do you know how to hold a crossbow? The son of William Tell probably knew well enough, but the artist who drew his picture on the low-value stamps of Switzerland, 1908, showed him holding the cord which is in front of the stock.  This cord should pass behind the stock, so the stamp was redrawn in 1910 to correct this. It is easy to distinguish these two varieties by the cord, but the stamp was redrawn again in 1911 to effect more subtle improvements. In this the lettering of " Helvetia " (Latin name for Switzerland) is quite different, and the little loop at the top of the bow is bolder and comes nearer the frame line under the letters VE. There was an earlier son of William Tell type in 1907, but it has an entirely different frame.

Our variety packet probably includes a few of the Transvaal stamps of the shield types of 1894–96. As first engraved, the Cape wagon which figures in the lower division of the shield was given two shafts instead of the single pole, or disselboom. The mistake was promptly noted by the public and only five denominations were printed with shafts. The die was re-engraved, the shafts being replaced by the pole. So the values ½d., 1d., 2d., 6d., and 1s. are each found in two varieties.

The French stamps in our packet will include some in the " sower " design which are liable to be passed over as duplicates. The design as first issued (1903) had a lined background, with the sun on the horizon. The light on the figure is not coming from the sun, but from some mysterious source in front of the figure. The design was altered in 1906—the background is now solid, the sun eclipsed, and only a small patch of ground is left for the sower to stand on.

So far the difference between the two engravings is plain enough, but in a third engraving, which appeared later in 1906, the lady is left without any ground to stand on. In 1907, in another re-engraving, the uncoloured numerals and the word " Postes " were made slightly bolder.

Many British Colonial stamps in the various key-plate designs have differences, prominent enough when you are looking for them, but liable to be overlooked by the beginner. The small inscriptions " Postage & Revenue " or " Postage-Revenue " have been interchanged with " Postage-Postage."

Where a country has retained a uniform style of design over a long period, there are nearly always variations which, while not immediately obvious, have to be noted by the collector. Norway has been faithful to its design featuring the numeral of value set in the ring of a posthorn. It appeared first as far back as 1871, when the old skilling currency was still in use. It was continued in the öre currency in 1877; it is still being used for some denominations to this day. To the general public the design appears the same all through, but the philatelist separates them into a range of different types, in the sequence of their redrawn and re-engraved forms.

It would not be convenient here to record all the varieties, but the chief changes may be briefly summarised:

1871. Original design, value in skilling. Posthorn shaded.
1877. As before, but value in öre.
1882. Posthorn not shaded.
1893. " Norge " is in new lettering, with serifs.
1910. White line of ring is not broken under the crown.
1917–29. New colours.
1937– . Printed by photogravure, slightly larger-sized stamps, with no vertical shading in the oval.
1962– . Recess-engraved.

It may sound rather complicated, but the difference between each successive modification is easily seen. You may have examples of each issue in the packet which is the nucleus of your collection, and you will want to know wherein they differ. It is a good exercise also for the use of your eyes in a more advanced stage of your collecting.

CHAPTER VII

CURIOSITIES OF PHILATELY

THERE IS A STRONG element of the curious and quaint in stamp collecting. We meet it in the diversified sizes and shapes of stamps, in paper and watermark, anachronisms and errors in design, freaks of design and engraving, errors and omissions in printing, crude productions that served as postage stamps, divisible stamps, stamps printed on both sides, and sometimes of different face value on one side from the other, typewritten stamps, stamps that contain secrets and puzzle pictures, trick stamps, and many more whose histories are unusual. There is much that is curious in connection with postmarks, and even forgeries.

Size.—Our present low-value stamps in current use are approximately ·85 inch × ·7 inch (as to image) and ·95 inch × ·8 inch from perforation to perforation. The image is only slightly smaller than that of the 1*d.* and 2*d.* stamps of 1840, which were ·9 inch × ·775 inch.

The smallest Great Britain stamp was the ½*d.* of 1870 (·55 inch × ·7 inch), while the £5 of 1882, at 1·2 inches × 2·15 inches, is the largest.

The world's smallest stamps are the three varieties of the 1863–66 issue of the State of Bolivar: 10 centavos green, 10 centavos rose, and 1 peso red. These are ·45 inch by ·4 inch. Bergedorf provides the earliest instance of stamps being graduated in size according to denomination from the small ½ schilling to the full-size 4 schillinge (1861).

The largest adhesive postage stamps were the 5, 10, and 25 cents newspaper and periodical stamps issued by the United States in 1865. They are 3·75 inches high by 2 inches wide, and were intended for use on packets of newspapers on which the postage was prepaid by publishers.

Shape.—There can be no doubt the creators of the first adhesive postage stamps of 1840 found the most convenient shape for the labels. Other shapes have been tried, but none has proved superior or even equal to it.

The first notable departure from the rectangular shape was the triangular form of the stamps of the Cape of Good Hope in 1853. This shape was determined upon to make the Colony's stamps quite distinctive from those of Great Britain, which were familiar on mail arriving in the Colony.

A similar reason for a distinctive shape caused Colombia to make its 2½ centavos stamps of 1865 and 1869 triangular. These stamps were issued to prepay delivery to the house or office of the addressee. Ordinary postage only paid the charge to the post office of destination, where the addressee had to call or send for mail. The little 2½ centavos triangles readily caught the sorters' attention to the fact that a special fee had been prepaid for delivery to the house. The 1865 stamp is an equilateral, but the 1869 is a scalene triangle. The latter, seen as a single specimen, looks an awkward shape for printing, but if you put two together with the longest dimensions meeting, the pair form a rectangle.

The Newfoundland 3d. green triangle of 1857 is one of three shapes (upright rectangle, square, and triangle) serving to differentiate the denominations.

Triangular stamps proved unsuitable when perforation came into general use, and most of them were discarded. In later times, triangles have returned, sometimes to serve as distinguishing features on letters requiring special service, but perhaps more often because the unusual shape piques the interest of the young stamp collector.

Many stamps are circular, oval, or irregular in the configuration of the design, but most of these are rectangular when perforated, and even the early imperforate circles and ovals were probably intended to be cut square, instead of being cut to shape. It seems to have been the common practice on the part of the public in British Guiana to cut the " circular " stamps of 1850 more or less to shape. They are rarely to be met with cut square. The same appears to have been largely the practice with the Afghanistan and the Kashmir (1866) circular stamps.

Among the great range of Russian Zemstvo (or Rural) stamps are a few which were actually punched out in circles or ovals, most of them plain edged, but some with scalloped edges. Among these rurals are diamond-shaped stamps, generally imperforate, but some perforated.

Diamond-shaped stamps were issued for Djibouti, 1894, (imperforate) and North Mongolia (Touva), 1927, perforated. Octagonal stamps perforated on all eight sides were issued by the Turkish Army of Occupation in Thessaly in the Græco-Turkish War of 1898. Similarly perforated octagonal stamps were used by Belgium in the telegraph service from 1871 onwards.

Double-sided Stamps.—It would surprise you to find that the penny stamps you had lately bought at the post office were fully printed on both sides. The long-familiar 1*d*. purple Queen Victoria stamp of 1881 exists with the full impression on front and back; sometimes both impressions are the same way up, while on others the impression on the back is upside down.

A long list could be drawn up of stamps printed on both sides. More unusual is it to find a stamp printed on both sides expressing a different denomination on one side from that on the other. A Mexican 1 real of 1861 is known with an impression of the 2 reales on the back, while Venezuela about 1880 had some which were 25 centimos yellow on the front and 5 centimos yellow on the back.

These and some of the other curios of stamp printing are

generally to be attributed to economy in the use of Government paper, every sheet of which a printer may have to account for. A sheet of stamps printed with insufficient colour had probably been turned over and printed on the other side of the paper. Occasionally a whole edition of a stamp which has been printed in too weak a colour has been printed again over the first colour, in a stronger colour. An instance occurred in Sweden about 1875 when an edition of the 20 öre pale orange stamp was printed again in vermilion. The second printing was so nicely adjusted to the first that it was many years before a stamp collector noted the circumstances of the double printing.

Back Views.—There are plenty of other strange things to be found on the backs of stamps. For many years Spanish stamps had numbers printed on the back; Sweden has had a posthorn printed on the back in lieu of a watermark in the paper. The St. Anthony of Padua stamps issued by Portugal in 1895 (700th anniversary of the birth of the Saint) have a kind of prayer printed on the back, an allusion to the " Solemnity of the Tongue." Some of the stamps of Fiume bear on the back the snake-and-stars badge of the Arditi.

The backs of stamps were used for commercial advertisements in New Zealand in 1893. At one time (1888) there was a proposal to use the backs of Great Britain stamps for a like purpose, the late Mr. John Barratt having offered a large sum for the privilege of advertising " Pears' Soap " on the backs of our $\frac{1}{2}d.$ and $1d.$ stamps. Some trials on the back of the $1d.$ lilac stamp are known with the name of this commodity in various colours.

Shortage of suitable paper has occasionally led to the printing of stamps on the plain side of paper already printed on one side with maps and bank-notes, as in Latvia.

Two of the old-time curiosities were purposely printed on the reverse or gummed side of thin transparent paper, in the manner of a mirror print. These were the 10 silbergroschen rose, and 30 silbergroschen blue stamps of Prussia, 1866. In these the printed side was meant to be affixed to packets when the design showed the correct way through the transparency. It was a patented idea for preventing stamps being used a second time. The paper is often described as goldbeater's skin.

.   .   .   .   .

Want of more suitable gummed paper for provisional stamps led the French postmaster at Zanzibar to print temporary denominations on the sheet and pane margins of French stamps, an expedient also used by a postmaster at Emory, Virginia, during the American Civil War.

Manuscript Surcharges.—It is a little mystifying that the stroke of a postal official's pen should alter the denomination of a stamp as in the 1d. on 6d. Trinidad 1882, the 1d. on half 6d. Tobago 1880, " One Dollar " on 16 cents Labuan 1883; it is still more curious to discover that a manuscript 1d. in red ink on a 4d. blue Cape of Good Hope makes it a stamp of Griqualand West, and to be found in your catalogues only under that heading.

The ubiquitous typewriter has been used to surcharge stamps (Tonga), and even to print stamps (Uganda).

Changeling Stamps.—There are numbers of stamps which might be classed as trick stamps. It is surprising what a bath will do to some stamps. When the ½d. Queen Victoria stamp was changed from its vermilion (1887) to green in 1900, people were continually finding specimens that were bright blue; plain water had changed them, and had a similar effect upon the first King Edward VII ½d. green stamp.

When the German liner, S.S. *Eider*, homeward bound from New York, was wrecked off the Isle of Wight on January 31st, 1892, the purser's stock of German stamps, after immersion in sea-water, showed a surprise disfigurement. The salt water had reacted on a secret underprint which had been printed in an invisible ink in which phenolphthalein was the chief constituent. Neither collectors nor the German public knew until then that the stamps they used were so protected; it was the carefully guarded secret of the Imperial State Printing Works.

. . . . .

The designs of stamps abound in curious and interesting details. The collector just glancing at the picture on a stamp may easily miss piquant features in the frame surround or background. You may find the artist's or engraver's initials or name on some. The engraver of the 1858 " Arms " stamps of Naples hid a different letter in the border of each of the seven dies for the seven denominations. The early collectors puzzled long over these tiny secret marks, but if you take the letters in their sequence from the $\frac{1}{2}$ to the 50 grana values, they spell out G. Masini.

The common Japanese stamps of 1876–77 look much the same in general design, and one is rather puzzled on looking closely into the spandrels to find there are different emblems for each value. In a land where the smallest details of the stamp designs are distinctively Oriental in character, it is curious to find three-fanned steamship propellers in the spandrels of the 6 sen, screw propellers on the 8 sen, horseshoe and whip on the 10 sen, and balloons on the 12 sen.

Look at the borders of the Pro Juventute stamps of Switzerland, and see how a frame of watches tells of the chief industry of Neuchâtel; similarly there are cog-wheels (Zürich), grapes (Vaud), pearl necklaces (Geneva), sailingships (Lucerne), and many more tiny devices well worth attention for the stories they have to tell us.

There are collectors who have been collecting for years who have missed most of these interesting little details. They have not used or developed their powers of observation.

CHAPTER VIII

ERRORS

Plate 4

STAMPS AFFORD ABUNDANT ILLUSTRATION of man's infinite capacity for making mistakes. The young Latinist may smile at the old lithographic draughtsman who rendered British Guiana's motto *Damus petimus que vicissim*, with the second word as *patimus*, on the first London-printed stamps for the colony, 1852. The two values are now rare, but they will probably always retain for collectors the popular description of the " Patimus Guianas."

What shall we say of the succession of lettered Frenchmen, from Monsieur le Ministre downwards, who passed the curious blunder on the scarlet 90 centimes stamp of 1937 issued in honour of Descartes? Here was an excellent portrait of the philosopher, his quill and inkwell by his side, and an open book bearing, incorrectly, the title of his most famous work. The title-page, curiously enough a left-hand page, reads *Discours sur la Méthode*, when nearly all good Frenchmen know Descartes gave it the title *Discours de la Méthode*.

The stamp appeared on June 10th, 1937, that being the 300th anniversary of the first publication of the work. A second and corrected edition was issued soon afterwards.

Artists' or engravers' errors of detail are numerous and provide some unexpected results. That a British Colony should present at the left-hand side of a stamp border the Union Jack flying upside down was a grave enough error to call for a corrected edition ($2\frac{1}{2}d$. Jamaica, February and November 1921). The frame of the $2d$. stamp of the same series shows bananas growing upwards.

One cannot expect artists to know everything, but when designing the first " Seal on Ice-floe " for Newfoundland, the seal was pictured with forepaws, instead of flippers. A zoologist may find artists slipping up on details of animals, and many a time an old or young salt has pointed out to me inconsistencies in maritime subjects; all these and many more slips in designing or engraving add spice to our scrutiny of things depicted on stamps. Anachronisms, or apparent anachronisms, like Christopher Columbus using a telescope on the St. Kitts-Nevis stamp, are rarely attributable to the stamp artist. Columbus with telescope or spy-glass has long figured as the badge of St. Christopher, and the stamp artist had to embody the colony's badge in the design.

More startling errors have occurred through confusion of subjects. The 2 cents United States 1912-13 stamp, one of the series issued to commemorate the opening of the Panama Canal, was originally described under the vignette as " Gatun Locks." Between 20 and 30 millions of this stamp had been printed when it was discovered that the view was not of Gatun, but of the Pedro Miguel Locks. The entire printing was destroyed, and after some months' delay the stamp with the same view, but discreetly labelled " Panama Canal," appeared in January 1913.

A similar class of mistake originating in the same printery, was the 18 cents vermilion pictorial stamp of the Philippine Islands, 1932. After issue, the view on this stamp described thereon as the Pagsanjan Falls was found to be a picture of the Vernal Falls in the Yosemite National Park, California. Although there was much talk of withdrawing the stamp and replacing it, no corrected edition was issued.

Errors of printing are not only numerous, but of very diversified character, and it is possible here to indicate only a few in each of the main groups.

Errors of Colour.—The most interesting examples of stamps

printed in colours not intended for them are caused when clichés or transfers get mixed up in assembling the printing forme or the lithographic stone. In early printings of the so-called " woodblock " triangular stamps, made locally in Cape Colony in 1861 from stereotypes mounted on a wooden base, one of the 1d. stereos got mounted among the 4d. stereos, while a 4d. likewise was mounted among the 1d. stereos. Thus on each sheet of red 1d. stamps there was one 4d. red error, and correspondingly the sheets of 4d. blue stamps each contained a 1d. blue error. Several printings were made of these stamps before the intrusive clichés were removed, the 1d. error being known in four shades of blue, and the 4d. in three shades of red. The original stereotypes are preserved in the Capetown Museum, and a photograph of them will be found on Plate 2.

These two errors of colour are of the highest degree of rarity unused, and are very rare in the used condition. Some interesting items preserved in a few great collections are pairs or blocks each showing an error *se tenant* with the normal stamp or stamps.

Instead of a cliché, as in typography, a lithographic transfer of a wrong denomination may intrude in a group of transfers laid down upon a lithographic stone. The intruding transfer results in a stamp of the wrong colour, as in the 50 centavos red (instead of green) Colombia of 1863. Two of the world's rarest stamps—the 2 reales blue (instead of red) Spain 1851 and the 180 centesimos dull red (instead of green) Uruguay of 1858—were caused in this way.

The same class of mistake can be laid down on a steel plate from a transfer roller, for line-engraving. A curious example is the 5 cents red (instead of blue) U.S. error of 1917; the explanation of occurrence will be found in Chapter XIII on United States stamps.

In a few cases printers have delivered full consignments

of a stamp in wrong colours. A new or a repeat order sent by cable, perhaps not too explicit, has led the printer to determine the colour. This happened with the 1s. orange-brown (instead of olive-yellow) Tobago, 1896.

Sometimes a plate for one stamp denomination is purposely printed in a colour not intended for that value, but to produce a distinctive surcharged provisional of another denomination. If a sheet so printed escapes the surcharge, the result is equivalent to an error of colour. In 1879 the 4d. South Australia, normally a purple stamp, was printed in deep ultramarine to be surcharged " 3 Pence." The deep ultramarine 4d. without the surcharge is a rarity of which fewer than a dozen copies are known.

Occasionally a sheet or two of proof sheets taken for colour have got into stock, perforated, and duly issued. This happened with three sheets of the 2½d. Great Britain Silver Jubilee stamps in 1935. The stamp is normally in an ultramarine blue, but three sheets printed in a distinct Prussian blue got into stock and were being sold at a suburban post office in London in June 1935 when a collector noticed their colour. He bought up all there were left, 316 out of the 360 (three sheets of 120). The catalogue price is now substantial.

Inverted Centres.—When stamps are printed in two or more colours, or at two or more operations, there is the liability that a sheet or two after being printed in one colour may be fed into the press the wrong way for the second impression. This kind of mistake produced what are the most interesting of stamp errors, the inverted centres.

The first stamp to get into circulation with the centre inverted was the famous Indian rarity, the 4 annas lithographed in blue and red at Calcutta in 1854. The Queen's head is in blue, and the frame in red. Although the inverted heads are of extreme rarity, the data collected of the few copies known show them to derive from at least three sheets. Of sixteen known copies, all save one are cut to shape.

British stamp printers have not made many inverted-centre errors for Commonwealth stamps. Throughout the whole range of Empire issues there are only fifteen. Of these, the " inverted swan " of Western Australia, 1854, was not caused by printing at two operations. The stamp was lithographed, in one colour at one operation; the stone was laid down with a paste-up of transfers consisting of separate frames and centres. In one case the two component parts of the transfer were relatively inverted, an accident not difficult to appreciate with such finicky work. A fine copy has sold for a little over £1,000, but few of the ten known copies are fine.

The United States " inverts " of 1869, of which two, 15 and 24 cents, are inverted centres and the 30 cents " inverted flags," are among the classic rarities. A block of four 24 cents with inverted centres escaped observation in Liverpool in the early 'nineties until a small dealer noticed and acquired it, selling it almost immediately for a mere £5 note. The next buyer sold it to an American collector, the late Mr. William Thorne, of New York, and later it passed into the W. H. Crocker (San Francisco) collection for £300. At the sale of the Crocker collection in London, November 1938, this fine block sold for £2,500.

Among the most celebrated errors of this class are the 12 cuartos rose and blue Spain, 1865, imperforate, and still rarer perforated. This is a case in which one can say definitely that the frame was inverted. One frame cliché used to form the border plate was set upside down. Consequently the head plate, bearing 100 profiles of Queen Isabella correctly set, produced one stamp to each sheet with the frame inverted.

A curious freak discovered in the 'nineties is the 50 bani red and blue stamp of Roumania of 1869, with Prince (afterwards King) Charles' head in the centre printed twice, one of the impressions being inverted. The second print of the head was probably an intended correction of the first, which was upside down.

Under the old Imperial régime in Russia the stamps were beautifully and most carefully printed. Errors were few and most of them very rare. The 10 and 20 kopecs of 1875–79, 14 and 20 kopecs, and 1 rouble, 1889–94, 14 and 35 kopecs, and 1, $3\frac{1}{2}$, and 7 roubles, 1902, and the 15 and 25 kopecs, 1905, all exist with inverted centres. Rather more of the stamps occur with inverted backgrounds; these are not very obvious, so one should look carefully at Russian stamps lest a rare variety gets past unnoticed.

Three old favourites which used to be inexpensive were the Quetzal stamps of Guatemala, 1881, with the bird upside down in its cage. The values are 2, 5, and 20 centavos, of which the 5 centavos is the rarest.

Some of the modern inverted centres are not so accidental as they appear. Are we to suppose that a great London firm of security printers making a series of thirteen denominations for Portuguese Nyassa in 1901 accidentally produced and passed nine of them as inverted-centre errors? The French Government printers did even worse in providing thirteen inverted centre varieties in the 1902 series for the French Somali Coast, and fourteen in the 1903 series. Where there is a strong suspicion of such errors being artificially produced, collectors are advised to leave them alone. They will prove dear at any price. The Nyassa giraffes were never planned to stand on their heads, and the mounted Somalis would have found their camels beyond their skill to ride topsy-turvy.

An exceptional class of error in bicoloured stamps is the

use of a wrong head plate or otherwise transposing the vignette for one denomination into the frame for another. The Panama Republic in 1909 issued a set of bicoloured stamps with portraits in the centres of all but one value. The stamps were used without overprint in the Republic, but those overprinted " Canal Zone " were for use in the territory controlled by the U.S.A. Among the overprinted stamps there exists as a rare error the 5 centesimos with the portrait belonging to the 2 centesimos. Only a few copies have been found, and so far no one has found the error without the Canal Zone overprint.

Errors of Omission.—Still among the stamps requiring two or more printings to complete them we find errors of omission. Stamps without their centres are curious objects, and the best-known one, the 1s. crimson Virgin Islands without the Virgin, is very highly prized. Yet it was never actually issued that way, and the copies known are really unfinished proofs.

Particularly among stamps printed on the key-plate system we find stamps from which the value has been omitted. They have missed the impression of the duty plate necessary to finish them. The 10 centimos carmine Queen's head stamp of Gibraltar, 1889, exists this way, and it is known that a sheet of these reached Gibraltar. In all probability it occurred through two sheets passing into the press together for the impression of the duty; the upper sheet was duly completed, while the under one escaped with only an albino impression of the duty plate.

Among other stamps known without their values, examples will be found in Gold Coast, Lagos, Trinidad, and Cook Islands, in the Portuguese Colonial key-plate types, and among the French Colonies some exist without the name of the colony inserted.

Errors of Inscription.—A real curiosity is a stamp of Sweden with one value " 20 " in figures and " Tretio öre " (thirty) in words. It is in vermilion, the colour appropriate to the 20 (tjugo) öre. Damage to a unit on the 20 öre plate was remedied by removing the defective cliché, and substituting a 30 öre cliché, altering the central figure from 30 to 20, but overlooking the fact that the value also appeared in words. These Swedish stamps were typographed, but a similar blunder was made in the first lithographed stamps of Lübeck. In laying down the stone for the 2 schillinge brown stamp, two transfers of the 2½ schillinge were used. To correct these the lithographer erased the " 2½ " from each of the four angles, and substituted the figures " 2," overlooking the value expressed in words " zwei ein halb " (Plate 14, Stamp 9).

British titles present difficulties to foreigners, as witness " Sir Codrington " on 5 drachmai Greece, 1927, later corrected to Sir Edward Codrington, but it was an English artist and lithographer who described Sir Francis Bacon as Lord Bacon on the 6 cents stamp of Newfoundland in 1910.

In some languages grammatical errors would come easy to an engraver not conversant with them. Two stamps of Bulgaria issued in 1885 have the inscriptions wrongly rendered in masculine when they should have been feminine: *edin stotink*, which is masculine, when it should have been the feminine *edna stotinka* for the 1 stot., and *dva stotinki* for *dve* on the 2 stot., *dva* being the masculine form, and *dve* the feminine. The stamps were re-engraved and issued in the correct form a year later.

The surcharging and overprinting of stamps yields the largest crop of printers' errors. After the explanations of mistakes already given in this chapter, it will not be necessary to explain how we get overprints inverted, sideways, double, and treble, on the wrong stamp or in the wrong colour. Where surcharges are hand stamped, inversion is so common as to be of small account.

Misprints in type-set overprints are more plentiful than amusing, but you may well be prepared to pay a little more for " Two Gents " than Two Cents (British Guiana, 1899), while it was not quite kind of the printer to antedate by ten years (on one stamp in each sheet) the wedding date of Lavinia and King George II of Tonga " 1 June 1889 " for 1899.

PART II
STAMPS OF THE WIDE WORLD

CHAPTER IX

GREAT BRITAIN

Plates 5 and 6

ON MAY 6TH, 1840, the first adhesive postage stamps were issued to the public throughout the British Isles. They were the 1d. black and the 2d. blue. Simple little rectangles of gummed paper, with a beautifully engraved profile of the young Queen Victoria, who had succeeded her uncle, William IV, to the throne just three years earlier. The Queen was twenty-one, but the stamp portrait follows that on a beautiful medal struck in the first year of her reign, when she was eighteen. For the next sixty years the Queen never aged—on her stamps. All the stamps of Great Britain to the end of her long reign bear the profile of the Queen as she was at her Accession. It was by her own wish in later years that the youthful portrait was retained all down the years.

During the Victorian era the British postage stamps fall into three main groups, distinguished by the methods of their manufacture: line-engraved, embossed, and typographed.

THE LINE-ENGRAVED SERIES.—The original 1d. and 2d. stamps of 1840 were printed from engraved steel plates, in the manner known as line-engraving. The collector will have no difficulty in recognising the " family resemblance " of the 1d. black, 1d. red, 2d. blue, the 1½d., and the midget ½d. stamps in use between 1840 and 1880. The resemblance is due to their sharing the same method of manufacture.

The 1d. and 2d. stamps were printed in sheets of 240 on paper which was watermarked so that each stamp has its small crown watermark. Each stamp on a sheet had a different combination of check letters in the lower corner squares. There were plate numbers in the margins of the sheet, but none on the stamps themselves until later. The stamps were imperforate, and had to be separated with scissors or knife.

The 1d. stamp made its bow to the public in black,

1840   1853
Small Crown
Watermarks

sombre perhaps, but see how finely black shows up the quality of the engraving. Within a year the black was discarded for a red 1d. stamp; the reason was that, the black being a fast ink, people found that they could wash off the postmarks and use the stamps again. From 1841 onwards to 1880 the 1d. stamps were all of a red colour, which had the advantage of showing up the postmarks better.

The 2d. blue, which came out along with the 1d. black, was continued in a blue colour right up to 1880, but it had a modification in its design, in 1841, in which white lines appear under the word "Postage" and over the "Two Pence."

The Check Letters.—The small capital letters in the lower corner squares were added by hand or by means of punches on the printing plate, and follow a regular plan. The 240 stamps were in twenty rows of twelve. In the left lower angle the letter denotes the horizontal row, while the right-hand corner letter indicates the vertical column. In each direction the sequence is strictly alphabetical. Thus a stamp lettered "A....A" was the first stamp (column 1) in the first row. This system, so far as it concerns the lower corners of the stamps printed 240 to the sheet, never varies, and consequently in the bottom left-hand corner the letter must always be anything from A to T (the twentieth row) and the right-hand bottom corner letter anything from A to L (the twelfth column).

To make this simple system perfectly clear here are a few examples:

1st row.—AA, AB, AC, AD, AE, AF, etc., to AL.

2nd row.—BA, BB, BC, BD, BE, etc., to BL.

10th row.—JA, JB, JC, JD, etc., to JK, JL.

20th row.—TA, TB, etc., to TH, TI, TJ, TK, TL.

The general collector does not collect all the 240 combinations of lettering on a particular stamp, but without an understanding of the system of the check letters, the novice is liable to regard them as different issues.

Perforation was introduced for our 1d. and 2d. stamps in 1854 (experiments had been going on since 1848), and at this period the old original Queen's head die was in need of renewal. A duplicate of it on steel was worked over by a skilled engraver, deepening the lines, and incidentally effecting some small but distinguishable differences. The original die (Die I) was retired and the re-engraved one (Die II, sometimes called Humphrys' Retouch) is the parent of subsequent plates. About the same time there was a change in the crown watermark device; instead of the small it is a large and more elaborate crown.

Remembering these changes in die, watermark, and the new convenience of perforation, we arrive at the long series of plate numbers showing on the actual stamps and having check letters in all four corners.

The check letters, now bolder, follow the same alphabetical plan in the lower corners as already described. The letters in the upper corners are the same as

1855   1861
Large Crown Watermarks

in the bottom corners, but in reverse order—thus a stamp with A....B in the lower corners has B....A in the top ones.

The stamps with letters in all four corners have tiny uncoloured figures in the interlaced lines of the inner frame at each side. These are the plate numbers.

Of the 1d. red stamp you may find the following plate numbers: 71 to 74, 76, 78 to 125, 127, 129 to 225. The printers only started this method of denoting the plate number with plate 69, and ended with plate 228; but 69, 70, 75, 77, 126, 128, 226, 227, and 228 were never used, though copies are known of plate 77, probably from proof sheets which may have been perforated in error and put into stock. Plate 225 is a scarce plate number worth searching for.

Of the 2d. blue stamp, the plate numbers to be found are: 7, 8, 9, 12, 13, 14, and 15.

A halfpenny rate for postage on inland postcards, inland newspapers, printed matter, patterns, and samples came into force on October 1st, 1870. On that date two new denominations were added to the line-engraved series—the

1d. and 2d.   ½d.   1½d.
Where to find the plate numbers

small ½d. and the 1½d., the latter in rose red, but having the head within a shield-shaped frame.

The ½d. stamp being just half the size of the 1d. stamps, there were 480 to the sheet instead of 240. Every stamp has check letters in all four corners, and a tiny white figure (the plate number) in the network at each side of the portrait oval. The plate numbers found are 1, 3 to 6, 8 to 15, 19 and 20. Plate 9 is the scarcest.

There being 480 stamps to the sheet, we should note (a)

that there is a special watermark, consisting of the words *half penny* in script, one complete watermark to every three stamps, and (*b*) the check letters go farther. The steel plate was turned on its long dimension, yielding twenty rows of twenty-four stamps, the first stamp being lettered $\frac{AA}{AA}$ and the last $\frac{XT}{TX}$.

Three-halfpence.—This denomination was printed, like the contemporary 1*d.* stamps, in sheets of 240, on the large crown watermark, and with check letters in all four corners. There are only two plates to consider; the first was not numbered on the stamps, and is identified as Plate 1 by the absence of any number. A second plate was made, but, being defective, it was never used. The only other plate for this stamp is numbered " 3 " in the network at the sides near the bottom corner squares.

On the first (the unnumbered) plate there occurred one of the few rare errors of the check-lettering, a stamp lettered $\frac{OP}{PC}$ instead of $\frac{CP}{PC}$. The error was the third (C) stamp in the P (sixteenth) row.

These Victorian era line-engraved stamps were all printed by the old firm of Perkins, Bacon & Co. at their works, then at 69 Fleet Street and Whitefriars Street. There were just these four denominations, but of them during the forty years 1840–80 the firm produced a grand total of 22,681,312,800 stamps. The original 1*d.* blacks accounted for 69 millions, and the original 2*d.* blues (before the " white lines " were cut) accounted for 6,864,000.

The four denominations in the line-engraved series were supplemented with other values printed elsewhere and by other methods.

THE EMBOSSED ADHESIVES.—As the Post Office concluded

postal conventions with other countries, the need then arose for stamps of other denominations. A 1s. stamp was required for postage on letters to the United States and to certain British colonies; a 10d. stamp was required for letters transmitted to France, and to several British colonies. These denominations were provided in 1847 by the simple but slow method of embossing dies one at a time on sheets of gummed paper. The embossing was done on the embossing presses at Somerset House, on paper known as Dickinson silk-thread paper, having continuous fine threads of coloured silk introduced (according to a prepared plan) in its substance. The same kind of silk-thread paper had been used for the Mulready envelopes and wrappers, and also for some of the embossed envelopes.

The 1s. stamps were printed in green, and the 10d. in brown. In each case a sheet was composed of twenty stamps in five rows of four, but as each stamp was struck separately, the spacing between the stamps is uneven, and occasionally stamps are met with the impressions overlapping.

In 1854 the lowering of some of the postal rates to European countries and the reduction of the registration fee to 6d. led to the issue of a 6d. mauve stamp, embossed like the 1s. and 10d., but on paper watermarked with thin capital letters " VR."

These are beautiful stamps, but the collector must be careful to preserve the embossing, which is liable to get flattened out unless protected from pressure with sunk cardboard mounts.

THE TYPOGRAPHED STAMPS.—The printing of our stamps by the old line-engraved method was slow, and mechanical invention during the nineteenth century failed to speed it up. There were many who considered that the stamps could be printed more expeditiously and economically by the typographic method, and still preserve equal security from counterfeiting. Another point which had much weight with the Inland Revenue authorities was the claim that the typographer had ampler means of using special precautions against the cleaning of stamps for re-use in the post.

Messrs. Thos. de la Rue & Co. were already printing fiscal stamps for the Inland Revenue by typography on an enamelled paper, when it was decided to try the typographic method for a new denomination, the 4*d*., issued in 1855. This was printed in deep carmine on a highly enamelled blue safety paper, watermarked " small garter," and later watermarked " medium garter." The stamps were not satisfactory—official trials found them to be cleanable with ease. Unfortunately for collectors the enamelling of the surface is often disintegrated, and examples in pristine condition are now scarce. Then the stamp was printed on white paper in a very fugitive rose carmine. This is a rarity with the small garter watermark, uncommon with the medium, but most accessible on a new paper with large garter.

In 1856 it was decided to supersede the embossed adhesives 6*d*. and 1*s*. (the 10*d*. was abandoned), and print them typographically. They come on paper watermarked " emblems," each stamp having four tiny watermarked devices—two roses, a thistle, and a shamrock.

From this time onwards all new denominations above the 2*d*. (which you will remember was line-engraved until 1880) are of the typographed class; they are met with on a variety of watermarked papers, and were subjected to more or less prominent modification; check letters added in 1862 were at first very tiny and " white," but from 1865 large, but still " white." There are indications for distinguishing some of the early plates, but from 1865 the plate number is to be seen on the stamps either at the sides of the frame or near the base.

It would be impossible here to describe all the varieties included in this group, which broadened out in 1880 to include all the Victorian British postage stamps from $\frac{1}{2}d$. to £5 to the end of the reign.

King Edward VII.—Nearly a year elapsed after the death of the Queen (January 22nd, 1901) before the first stamps of the new reign appeared on New Year's Day, 1902. All the stamps of the reign are typographed, and most of the designs are similar to those of the last Victorian issue, which had become almost monotonously familiar to the public in the years from 1887 to 1901. The King's head was specially drawn for the stamps by the late Emil Fuchs, who also did the coinage heads.

All the stamps up to 1s. were uniform in size, and have a watermark known as " Imperial Crown." The 2s. 6d., 5s., and 10s. are larger, and have an anchor for watermark, while the highest value, the £1, is a long oblong, about equal to a strip of three normal stamps, and its watermark consists of three crowns. There had been a £5 stamp in Queen Victoria's time, and one was prepared, but not issued, with King Edward's head.

Stamp booklets were introduced in this country early in King Edward's reign (1904), and as the manufacture of these requires a special plate lay-out, a brief reference to it here will explain why the $\frac{1}{2}d$. and 1d. stamps are so commonly encountered with the watermark inverted. The ordinary sheet stamps of low values were of 240, in two panes (one above the other) of 120.

For the booklets there were still 240 to the sheet, but in four panes of sixty, there being a centre margin running down the sheet as well as across it. Each pane of sixty stamps has its first three columns the right way up, but its fourth, fifth, and sixth columns have the stamps upside down. Naturally, the upside-down stamps have the watermark inverted.

By laying on the printed back cover card (forty-set) sheets of stamps so laid out, with interleaving sheets, and front cover card (forty-set) the whole thickness is stitched or wired, in four vertical directions, once at each side margin and twice down the middle panel margin. Now a guillotine cutter slices the mass across at every second row, ten cuts giving us ten strips of four little booklets, which are then cut apart into single booklets. That additional margin down the centre has provided the binding strips for the booklets on its immediate left and right, while the outer side margins take the stitching for the rest. Thus forty little booklets are worked at one time, and 50 per cent. of the stamps issued in booklets have the watermark inverted. Naturally, such varieties are common, but many beginners noticing them fancy they have discovered something rare and " un-catalogued."

The British stamp contract passed to new printers, Messrs. Harrison & Sons, Ltd., as from January 1st, 1910, and this firm continued to print most of the Edwardian stamps (with some exceptions printed at Somerset House) until they were ready with the new stamps for the next reign.

King George V.—The change of stamp printers, combined with new arrangements by which the Royal Mint had charge of the provision of dies and plates, delayed the issue of the first Georgian stamps until Coronation Day, June 22nd, 1911. Only the $\frac{1}{2}d.$ and 1d. stamps were ready, and they were disappointing. The royal profile taken from a photograph was a failure; the naval suggestion in the dolphins of the $\frac{1}{2}d.$ frame was liked, but the engraving was poor; and an animal-loving public found the lion on the 1d. stamp to be a travesty of the king of beasts.

Officialdom, slow to admit failure, had the original dies .

tinkered up, giving us two dies of each of these first $\frac{1}{2}d$. and 1d. This was only a slight opening-up of the dies to improve their reproductive quality. Still the stamps were poor, and much abused. Then a further attempt to improve the engraving of the head and to fatten up the starved lion was made. More than a year passed before the authorities realised the stamps were fundamentally bad, and set about making a new start. Meanwhile Edwardian stamps were still being used for all values except the $\frac{1}{2}d$. and 1d.

The new start expressed itself in the new 1d. scarlet stamp of October 1912, with the head engraved from a specially prepared portrait by Mr. (afterwards Sir) Bertram Mackennal, the sculptor. The frame also was of his designing. The two earlier frames were both by Mackennal, and the dolphins frame was used for some values in the new series; the lion was released, and disappeared.

All these stamps were typographed, and the designs prevailed throughout the reign. The higher values, 2s. 6d., 5s., 10s., and £1, were line-engraved in a fine design by Mackennal, introducing, in addition to the royal effigy, the figure of Britannia in a chariot drawn by sea-horses. These stamps were successively printed by four great printing firms from 1913.

Messrs. Waterlow & Sons secured the contract for the typographed low values from 1924 to 1934. During this period there were two exceptional issues, one in 1924–25 marking the British Empire Exhibition at Wembley in those years. The other, in 1929, celebrated the holding in London of the Ninth Congress of the Universal Postal Union. This set is remarkable for the beautiful large engraving of the £1 black.

The return of the main contract to Messrs. Harrison & Sons in 1934 was a prelude to the adoption of the modern process of rotary photogravure. In my opinion it was a pity not to change the designs with the introduction of the photogravure stamps, for they had been drawn to suit a different method of printing.

The Silver Jubilee stamps of May 1935, four low values, were rather a startling departure as to design for our stamps, but perhaps represented fairly enough the days of flagpoles, bunting, and illuminations.

King Edward VIII.—There were but four adhesive postage stamps of the short reign, all in one simple unadorned design. The photographic origin of the profile was appropriate here, as it was to be reproduced in the photogravure manner.

The watermark follows the Roman letter style, but instead of the Roman VIII the figure " 8 " was used, thus E 8 R (see Chapter XVI). Although not all issued during this reign, eight of the postage due stamps were printed on this paper.

King George VI.—The late King succeeded on his brother's Abdication in December 1936. The first stamps of the new reign ($\frac{1}{2}d.$, 1d., and 2$\frac{1}{2}d.$) were in a design by Eric Gill, and bore a portrait by Edmund Dulac. They were printed by photogravure. A large 1$\frac{1}{2}d.$ Coronation stamp was issued, designed by Mr. Dulac, bearing for the first time in the history of Great Britain stamps portraits of the King and the Queen.

On May 6th, 1940, six attractive low-value stamps were issued in commemoration of the centenary of the first adhesive stamps. They depicted the head of Queen Victoria as shown on the Penny Black and the head of King George VI.

During 1941–42 the $\frac{1}{2}d.$ to 3d. values of the general issue reappeared in lighter shades to save ink, and by this time other values up to 1s. had been prepared. Recess-printed high values were issued in two different sets during King

George VI's reign, the 1951 2s. 6d. and 5s. stamps showing respectively H.M.S. *Victory* and the White Cliffs of Dover.

From 1946 to 1951 there were a number of special issues, in photogravure, commemorating Victory, the Royal Silver Wedding, the 1948 Olympic Games, the 75th Anniversary of the U.P.U., and the Festival of Britain.

Queen Elizabeth II.—Several artists were called upon to prepare designs for the general issue of the new reign, and, in addition, four attractive Coronation stamps were put on sale. Since then there have been many commemorative issues, and in 1958 special regional stamps appeared for Guernsey, Isle of Man, Jersey, Northern Ireland, Scotland, and Wales.

Official Stamps.—At the time the 1d. black stamp was issued in 1840 a plate (240-set) was made showing the letters VR instead of the star ornaments in the top corners. It was intended to use this VR stamp on correspondence of Government Departments, but the idea was abandoned. Although never put into use, the stamp is found in many collections unused, and sometimes with experimental cancellations. In all respects except the top corner letters, the stamp is like the ordinary 1d. black, but much scarcer.

Between 1880 and 1904 contemporary British postage stamps, Queen Victoria and King Edward VII types, were overprinted for use on official mail, the overprint indicating the particular department, except in the case of " Govt. Parcels." These departments were: " I.R. Official," Inland Revenue; " Army Official," War Office; " O.W. Official," Office of Works; " Board of Education "; " R.H. Official," Royal Household; " Admiralty."

British stamps surcharged with foreign currencies were for use in British post offices abroad, chiefly in the Levant (paras and piastres) and in Morocco (centimos and pesetas, centimes and francs).

CHAPTER X

THE COMMONWEALTH OVERSEAS

THE FIRST OVERSEAS POSSESSION of the British Commonwealth to issue postage stamps was the remote colony of Mauritius. Its first two stamps, 1*d*. orange-red and 2*d*. deep blue, issued September 1st, 1847, were locally engraved in imitation of the contemporary stamps of the Mother Country.

The portrait of the Queen is not flattering, but at the base of the neck the engraver put his initials, J. B. He was Joseph Barnard, watchmaker and jeweller at Port Louis, the chief town. He had had no special training as an engraver, and no facilities other than his watchmaker's hand tools. Even the copper plate on which he engraved the two heads had been used before—on one side it had a local hotel's advertisement. This, turned over and polished, provided the plate from which the two famous rarities were printed, one at a time.

The two stamps are readily distinguishable from similar designs used later, for on the left side, reading upwards, are the words " Post Office." In the next issue the inscription reads " Post Paid." These two stamps of 1847 are among the best-known rarities of philately. Twenty-five copies, about equally divided between the two values, are recorded, and of these eight are definitely " off the market," being either in the Royal Collection or various national collections.

It will be obvious that these first stamps of the overseas possessions must be counted out for the average collector. There is no lack of interest for all in the later issues of the colony in the Queen's-head period, and in the Arms designs, the shield of which illustrates the motto *Stella clavisque maris indici,* the star and key of the Indian Ocean. The appearance of an unfamiliar face on a 15 cents ultramarine in 1899 reminds us that the island once belonged to France; the picture shows Admiral Mahé de La Bourdonnais, who was French Governor in the early eighteenth century.

The Seychelles, a large group of islands in the Indian Ocean, were administered from Mauritius and used that colony's stamps until 1890, when the dependency was provided with Queen's-head stamps. Different pictorial sets were issued in 1938 and 1952 bearing King George VI's head; in 1954 and 1962 there were Queen Elizabeth II issues.

Among British East African countries the early issues rejoice in a plethora of surcharges for B.E.A. and Zanzibar, but since 1896 the latter protectorate, with its gallery of portraits of successive Sultans, has had some of the most handsome of stamps. The first Uganda stamps (1895–96) were made by an English missionary at Mengo on a typewriter, and denominated in the native shell currency of cowries. Later a small printing press enabled another missionary to print type-set stamps, which took the Indian currency of annas and rupees. Kenya, Uganda, and Tanganyika (Tanzania) occasionally share commemorative issues, but each also have their own definitives.

The Somaliland Protectorate in the Queen Elizabeth II series had among other designs the Somali Rock pigeon, the Martial eagle and the Blackhead sheep.

The old stamps of British Central Africa, with the shield designed by that versatile genius, the late Sir H. H. Johnston, gave way to stamps of the Nyasaland Protectorate, the Rhodesia and Nyasaland Federation and now, Malawi.

The Sudan camel stamps have long been favourites, and other designs of this former Anglo-Egyptian Condominium paid tribute to the great General Gordon.

The Union of South Africa, established in 1910, brought to a close the separate stamp issues of four great colonies which had long been prominent in the world of stamps. These were the Cape of Good Hope, Natal, the Transvaal, and the Orange River Colony.

The Cape of Good Hope is in the forefront of philatelic favour, its early triangular stamps holding an unchanging attraction for collectors. The stamps in this unusual shape fall in three groups. The first, issued in 1853, were line-engraved by Perkins, Bacon & Co., in London. The second comprise the two values manufactured locally by typography in crude imitation of the original design; these are the so-called " woodblocks " (see Plate 2 and Chapter XIX) and the famous errors of colour. The third and last stage of the three-cornered Capes came in 1863–64, when De la Rue & Co. printed new supplies from the original engraved plates in colours rather brighter than those used by Perkins, Bacon & Co.

From 1864 the rectangular " Hope-seated " design dominates the issues until the King Edward VII reign, when " Hope " resigned.

Natal entered the stamp arena in 1857 with some unprepossessing locally made stamps embossed without ink on different-coloured papers. In 1859 a lovely full-face portrait of the Queen, line-engraved, was used for a few years, and the later issues include some pleasing Queen's-head designs in typography.

The Transvaal issues trace the history of the colony from the first South African Republic, through the first British occupation, the second republic, to the second occupation and annexation as a colony in the closing days of the Victorian reign. The Orange River Colony stamps, with the orange trees and bugles design, follow a similar course, the changes being noted chiefly in surcharges.

In southern Africa are many lands whose stamps present abundant general as well as philatelic interest. Basutoland (now Lesotho) depicted a crocodile sporting on a river bank, but there are no crocodiles in the country itself. Bechuanaland (now Botswana) depicted its cattle and the baobab tree, and like the other territories concerned, celebrated philatelically the Royal visit of 1947.

The first half-century since the British South Africa Company got its charter has witnessed vast developments in the country named Rhodesia after that great empire-builder Cecil Rhodes, who appeared on the 1½d. value of a series issued in 1940 to commemorate the Golden Jubilee of the Company.

The earliest issues from 1890 to 1925 showed the Company's arms, and later the Victoria Falls, a double-portrait issue of King George V and Queen Mary, and finally one of the most attractive stamp portraits of the late King George V as an admiral. This portrait was continued by Southern Rhodesia (south of the Zambezi River) when it was given separate government in 1923; this colony produced some pleasing stamps during the reigns of King George VI and Queen Elizabeth II; particularly attractive was the 1953 set commemorating the centenary of Cecil Rhodes' birth. Northern Rhodesia, which embraces the provinces north of the Zambezi, is now called Zambia and has various pictorial stamps.

The stamps of the Union of South Africa and its mandate South West Africa were linguistic curiosities. In the sheets of stamps as printed, the inscriptions were alternately in English and Afrikaans. Many collectors like to take them in pairs. A gold-mine, with sample streaks of glitter, was a novel picture on a 1½d. grey-green and gold South Africa, 1936; many other local scenes and subjects are pictured on the Union stamps and those of the mandate territory, including special issues in 1952 to celebrate the Van Riebeeck tercentenary. South Africa is now a republic.

Swaziland for a spell had its name overprinted on stamps of the second South African Republic (1889–95). After a long interval the British Protectorate was provided with its own stamps, and it is now a Protected State.

Zululand first had Great Britain stamps overprinted with her name, 1888–93, then Natal stamps similarly treated, 1894. Finally a Queen's-head key-plate design provided a series from ½d. to £5 in 1894; these were superseded by Natal stamps when Zululand was annexed to the old colony, 1897.

The West African countries follow in their stamps the political and economic rise of Nigeria, now embracing Lagos, as well as the former Southern and Northern Nigerias. Of earlier philatelic fame there are also Sierra Leone, Gambia, and Gold Coast (nowadays Ghana). Sierra Leone has given us a fine pictorial series, designed by a priest, and issued in honour of the centenary of the abolition of slavery and of the death of William Wilberforce. Gambia's most interesting stamps are the early embossed cameos in use from 1869–97.

St. Helena has had its own stamps from 1856. Ascension, which was administered by the Admiralty as if it were a ship until 1922, is now an annex of St. Helena, but with its separate stamps. There was a new birds series in 1963.

Canada, not yet a Dominion, issued her first stamps in 1851 in pence currency. The three designs show a beaver in its native haunts (3d.), a portrait of Prince Albert (6d.), the consort of Queen Victoria, who herself figures on the "twelve pence" black stamp, the classic rarity among Canadian issues. The term "shilling" was not appropriate here, as the pence were currency pence, of which twelve equalled 10d. sterling. A 10d. stamp added in 1855 introduced a portrait of Jacques Cartier. In 1859 the decimal coinage was adopted, and the old designs were revised for the cents series.

From the constitution of the Dominion (1867) onwards there is a grand range of beautifully engraved stamps through the successive reigns. There is the novel map stamp of " Xmas 1898," whose purpose was not so much to boast, " We hold a vaster Empire than has been," as to proclaim the great boon of Imperial Penny Postage introduced at that time.

The Dominion absorbed former colonies, and its stamps superseded the beautiful old stamps of New Brunswick, Nova Scotia, and later those of Prince Edward Island, British Columbia, and Vancouver Island.

Although previous provision was made for the admission of Newfoundland to the Dominion of Canada, our oldest colony retained separate identity and stamps till 1949. Starting in 1857 with finely engraved stamps in designs showing emblems of the Mother Country, they ranged through a pictorial variety of the colony's resources (seal, cod, salmon, etc.), a regular gallery of Royal Family portraits, historical scenes, and local scenery, and gave particular attention to the colony's associations with the progress of transatlantic flight.

Our one colony in Central America, British Honduras, has issued stamps since 1866, and has rejoiced in pictorial series of scenes, including representations of Maya antiquities and of that peculiar animal, the armadillo.

South America also holds one British colony, and that one the El Dorado of the stamp hunter. British Guiana has produced more of the capital rarities among stamps than any other country. Its first stamps were set up in type within circular rules in a local newspaper office in Georgetown in 1850. They are printed in black on coloured paper. Of the 2 cents, on rose-tinted paper, only three pairs and four single copies are known to collectors. One of the pairs has sold at auction for no less than £5,250. The other values, 4 cents, 8 cents, and 12 cents, are all of a high degree of rarity.

Even these are exceeded in scarcity by the type-set stamps of 1856. The 1 cent black on magenta paper is only known in one copy; the colony, and indeed the world, has been searched for a second specimen, without result. After resting in one great collection in Paris from 1878 to 1922, it came up at auction in that year and city, where it was sold for £7,343.

The 4 cents stamp of the same type of 1856 exists in black on magenta, on rose carmine, and on blue surface-coloured papers, all rarities, but rarest of all the 4 cents is one on blue sugar paper, coloured blue throughout, and which was the kind of blue paper in which the colony's Demerara sugar was packed.

Apart from the great rarities, there is a wide range of interesting stamps of this colony. Since independence in 1966 the country has become known as Guyana, and under this title has issued new definitive stamps and various commemoratives, including two which show the famous 1 cent black on magenta of 1856.

The British island colonies of the West Indies form one of the most popular Commonwealth groups among collectors. They are too numerous to attempt to describe in any detail here, but each is capable of providing deep technical interest for the specialist and ample pictorial charm for the general collector. In the case of the Leeward Islands colony there were two stamp issues in concurrent use in each Presidency. The stamps inscribed "Leeward Islands" were valid in all, but in addition Antigua, St. Kitts-Nevis (now re-named St. Christopher, Nevis and Anguilla), Dominica, Montserrat, and the Virgin Islands have separate sets of their own.

The Windward Islands have no collective series, but Grenada, St. Vincent, and St. Lucia have their several issues.

Jamaica and her dependencies, the Cayman Islands, and the Turks and Caicos Islands, all have their own stamps, as also do the colonies of the Bahamas, Barbados, and Trinidad (with Tobago).

The North Atlantic island colony of the Bermudas had a primitive stamp devised by the Postmaster from his date stamp as early as 1848.

Away in the far south, off the Argentine Coast, is the colony of the Falkland Islands, famed in modern history for the great sea-battle of Coronel, and for associations with British exploration in Antarctica. These were reflected in pictorial stamps. The battle memorial is seen on the 2d. 1938, and there are pictures of the Royal Research Ships *William Scoresby* and *Discovery II*.

In 1944 these stamps were overprinted for use in the Falkland Islands dependencies of Graham Land, South Georgia, South Orkneys, and South Shetlands. Definitive issues were replaced by British Antarctic Territory stamps, except South Georgia which has its own issues.

Asia, with its vast Indian Empire, Ceylon, many Malayan possessions, and protected States, as well as others in Arabia and China, presents a very wide field to the stamp collector.

The first stamps issued in British India were small embossed circular labels like the old-fashioned " wafers " introduced in the province of Scinde in 1852. These gave way to the first Indian general issue under the régime of the East India Company—Queen's-head stamps lithographed in Calcutta in 1854–55. The London de la Rue firm started printing the Indian postage stamps in 1855 for the Company and continued later under the Crown (1860) and the Imperial administration 1877, right on to 1926, when India set up its own printing establishment, the Nasik Security Press, near Bombay.

For very many years the British Indian stamps bore only the profile of Queen-Empress or Emperor. Pictorial designs first appeared in 1931, and the stamps of King George VI depicted methods of mail transport in India from the dak runner to the aeroplane. After India achieved Dominion status in 1947 other stamps were put on sale—Mahatma Gandhi appeared on some—and India became a republic in 1950.

Under special conventions, all similar in terms, the states of Chamba, Faridkot, Gwalior, Jind, Nabha, and Patiala formerly had Indian stamps with their respective names overprinted supplied to them; these were valid for all purposes of the inland post until 1951. The stamp catalogues class these as the Convention States.

There is much weird fascination in the special stamps of the Native States, many of them native made.

The first stamps of Pakistan were Indian issues over-printed, but afterwards pictorial series appeared, including a view of the Khyber Pass. Attractive general and official series also appeared for Bahawalpur.

Ceylon is famous in the stamp world for its beautifully engraved early " pence " issues before the colony changed to the Eastern dollar currency. The modern pictorials show the tapping of rubber, plucking of tea, rice fields, the " Temple of the Tooth," and other island views. The Maldive Islands, formerly a dependency of Ceylon, had a separate issue, and became a republic in 1953.

Closely associated in their philatelic history, as well as in their political, postal, and economic development, the British colonies and settlements in Malaya have nevertheless seen complicated changes philatelically. They now form part of the Malaysian Federation which includes North

Borneo (now Sabah) and Sarawak. Brunei and Singapore have their own stamps. The Japanese occupying forces, 1942–44, left their mark philatelically.

Hong Kong stamps, standard typographed Queen's and King's heads, derived an immense interest among philatelists through their widespread use throughout the Treaty Ports of China and elsewhere in the Far East, such use being determinable by the postmarks. Charming photogravure-printed definitives were issued in 1962.

In the nearer East the changes wrought by the 1914–18 war were largely responsible for extending the number of British stamp-issuing spheres to Palestine, Transjordan (which became independent in 1946), Iraq (including the provisional issues of Baghdad and Mosul), Bahrain, Kuwait, and a few more. Aden, now independent, became a colony on April 1st, 1937, and besides producing stamps from that year, separate issues also arrived later from the Kathiri State of Seiyun and the Qu'aiti State.

In Australia, New South Wales was a few days ahead of Victoria in issuing its home-made stamps in 1850. Three local engravers, Robert Clayton, John Carmichael, and H. C. Jervis, shared in the engraving and re-engraving of those favourite first issues, originally called " gold diggings," but now commonly known as Sydney Views. The scene is an imaginary one, copied from the seal of the colony. The device originated with Josiah Wedgwood, to whom some Australian clay had been sent. The famous potter modelled a medallion emblematic of the new settlement, showing Hope seated welcoming Peace, Art, and Labour to Sydney Cove.

Following the Sydney Views came hand-engraved "laureated" Queen's-head stamps, and subsequently finely engraved stamps were obtained from London. One of the loveliest of these is the 5s. violet coin design, 1861–97.

Victoria's first stamps (1850) were lithographed in Melbourne, from a die engraved by a local engraver. They are known as the "half-length Queens," showing Her Majesty seated, holding orb and sceptre. Queensland and South Australia started off with beautiful line-engraved stamps obtained from London, all Queen's heads; Western Australia also sent to London for her first stamp, but represented upon it was the colony's emblem of the black swan. Tasmania started with home-made Queen's heads and bearing the old name Van Diemen's Land.

All these colonies were merged in the Commonwealth of Australia, whose stamps since 1913 have been used throughout Australia. The first Commonwealth design consisted of a barren-looking Australia with a single kangaroo on it. This was retained in use for some values for many years, supplemented by values in a King's-head design with kangaroo, emu, and wattle blossom. Later issues have brought more of the fauna and flora on to the stamps, and some handsome commemorative issues have appeared, notably for the opening of the Parliament House, Canberra, the centenaries of Western Australia, Victoria, and South Australia, and the sesquicentenary of the first settlement in Australia at Sydney Cove. The great single-span bridge over Sydney Harbour is seen on a few stamps issued to celebrate the opening in 1932.

New Zealand opened its postage series in 1855 with the line-engraved " full-face Queens " from plates engraved in London, and after the rare London prints most of the stamps were printed in the colony. The middle period in New Zealand stamps is not particularly attractive (the 5d. 1891 is almost a caricature), but the Dominion has made up with many beautiful stamps since. London landmarks appearing on New Zealand stamps have included the Peter Pan statue and, in 1953, Buckingham Palace and Westminster Abbey.

In the Pacific Ocean are numerous archipelagos of
romance, brought home to us on the colourful stamps of
Papua and New Guinea, British Solomon Islands, Nauru
(" Pleasant Island "), the Cook Islands, Fiji, Gilbert and
Ellice Islands, the New Hebrides (a Franco-British Con-
dominium), Samoa (with Vailima, the last resting place
of Robert Louis Stevenson) and Tonga, the " Friendly
Islands." Tokelau Islands issued their first stamps in 1948.

The first issue of Pitcairn Islands, famous for their
association with the mutiny on the *Bounty*, appeared in
1940 with a variety of designs, the 2d. showing the ship and
the redoubtable William Bligh.

Eire, formerly the Irish Free State, had her first separate
issue of stamps overprinted in Erse on Great Britain stamps
in 1922. Since then she has contrived a series of her own
design. The low values are in four designs, showing the
Sword of Light, an outline map, the heraldic shield, and a
celtic cross; the high values, 2s. 6d., 5s., and 10s. bear a
picture of St. Patrick. Some later stamps depict Daniel
O'Connell, the Shannon Barrage, a player of hurley, and
Thomas Moore. The bicentenary of the Guinness Brewery
was the occasion of an issue in 1959. Eire became completely
independent in 1949.

British stamps were used in the old Turkey from the time
of the Crimean War; from 1885 our stamps were surcharged
in Turkish currency (paras and piastres) and later overprinted " Levant " for use in British post offices in the
Ottoman Empire. Other Powers enjoyed similar privileges,
under the treaty of Capitulations, of establishing their own
post offices in Turkey, where most people preferred to trust
their correspondence to a British, French, or Austrian post
office rather than to the dilatory and insecure Ottoman
posts. When Turkey entered the 1914–18 war the Capitulations were abolished, but a few post-war British Levant

stamps appeared during 1921. A similar use of overprinted British and Gibraltar stamps was made in the Morocco Agencies, all of which are now closed.

Old island colonies in the Mediterranean—Gibraltar, Malta, and Cyprus—have had scenic stamps. The great rock fortress is seen from various angles; Malta takes us back through her historic associations, even to Biblical times, as represented in the pictures of the shipwreck of St. Paul. Cyprus also presents a postage-stamp panorama of her long history. It is now independent. The Ionian Islands were British at the time the stamps with the Queen's head in a garter frame were used there, from 1859 until 1864, when the group was ceded to Greece. The stamps bear no inscription of denomination, but are differentiated by the colours, orange, blue, and carmine respectively for the $\frac{1}{2}d$., 1d., and 2d. These are stamps which are much rarer used than unused, and the collector has to be wary of counterfeit postmarks.

From time to time general issues have appeared for the colonies, each colony having the same designs but with, of course, the name of the country different. They include the Coronation issues of 1937 and 1953, and the Victory, Silver Wedding, and U.P.U. 75th anniversary sets.

Stamps were issued in the Channel Islands during the German occupation, 1941–44. Guernsey had a set with $\frac{1}{2}d$., 1d., and $2\frac{1}{2}d$. values printed on the island, and British 2d. stamps of various kinds were also bisected and used for penny postage. Jersey had two issues, one an Arms type, and the other a crude pictorial set, the latter printed in Paris. In 1948 special 1d. and $2\frac{1}{2}d$. stamps of Great Britain to commemorate the liberation were prepared principally for Channel Islands use. Guernsey and Jersey now have 3d. and 4d. " regional " stamps.

CHAPTER XI

EUROPEAN STATES AND THEIR COLONIES

Plates 11 to 19

THE STAMPS OF THE Powers and nations of Europe and their respective possessions overseas can trace for us the chequered history of a hundred years of European civilisation. It has already been noted that the Swiss cantons of Geneva, Zürich, and Basle were early followers in 1843–45 of the plan of prepayment by means of adhesive stamps. The cantonal stamps gave way to those of the Swiss Confederation in 1850. The grandeur of the Alpine scenery is reflected in many of the stamps, but also the part this great little country has played as the central pivot of great international enterprises like the Universal Postal Union, the League of Nations, and the International Labour Bureau.

The early stamps of France (head of Ceres) followed soon after the fall of Louis Philippe, and mark the short-lived Provisional Republic of 1848–52. They gave way to the first portrait stamps of Louis Napoleon as President in 1852, to be superseded by the stamps of the Second Empire in 1853. These still bore the head of Napoleon III, and later (1862) were crowned with laurels of victory. The stamps of all these issues are typographed.

The Third Republic and its successors, from 1870 to the present time, have used stamp designs chiefly of agricultural and peaceful themes, like the Sower, but latterly many French celebrities from Joan of Arc to M. and Madame Curie, the discoverers of radium, have been depicted.

The stamp collector gets a better idea than most people have of the ramifications of the overseas territories of the French Republic. A general issue of stamps for use in the colonies in 1859 has been followed by numerous series for the separate colonies in which one can trace the development, the grouping, and regrouping of possessions and mandates in Africa, Asia, South America, the West Indies, and Oceania covering not far short of 5,000,000 square miles. The early stamps of the older possessions include some great rarities, e.g. the first Réunions, and the later issues of most French colonials are rich in pictures of native races and their habitations.

The little principality of Monaco rejoices in its own stamps, popular with collectors. Andorra, which got along very well without stamps of its own until 1928, now has two series in concurrent use, one provided by Spain, the other by France, the joint suzerains of the Valleys.

The disturbed history of Spain has been written in her stamps since Queen Isabella II appeared on the first issue of 1850. As revolutions changed régimes, so they changed the stamps: the issues of the Carlists 1873–74 were few, but historic, and have their modern but more prolific counterparts in the stamps of both sides engaged in the terrible civil war that started in Spain in 1936. One of the most piquant of Spanish issues in the reign of Alfonso XIII was that of 1905, consisting of ten values, each bearing a different scene from " Don Quixote."

The Spanish overseas colonies have diminished since the Spanish-American War, but there are still separate issues for the Spanish Sahara (including the former colonies of Cape Juby, La Aguera, and Rio de Oro). Spanish Guinea (which incorporates Elobey-Annobon-Corisco) no longer issues stamps. Fernando Poo now has its own stamps again, as do Rio Muni and Ifni.

From 1853 to 1880 the Portuguese stamps of Queen Maria, King Pedro V, and King Luiz were embossed, the heads being so heavily struck that sometimes they drop out of their coloured frames. From 1880 the stamps were generally typographed (but are now lithographed) at the Lisbon Mint. The King Manoel portrait had only just been printed in 1910 when revolution sent him to refuge in England, and the stamps with his portrait were overprinted with the word Republica.

Portugal retains a widely scattered empire in Africa, Asia, and Oceania, with separate stamps for Angola, Cape Verde, Mozambique, Portuguese Guinea, S. Tomé and Principe, Macao, and Timor.

A very talented English engraver, J. H. Robinson, engraved the steel dies for the fine portrait stamps of Leopold I of Belgium. These are known as the " Epaulettes," 1849, and the " Medallions," 1850. There is little to charm us in the stamps of the reign of Leopold II, but much of interest in the reign of the popular war hero, Albert I. The portrait of the latter in the war-time " tin hat " (series of 1919–20) is a general favourite. At one time there were excessive issues of charity and pseudo-charity stamps, which tended to diminish collectors' interest.

Belgian Congo stamps were among the most attractive scenic issues, and were in the first instance derived from an elaborate diorama by R. Mols and P. van Engelen, exhibited at the Antwerp Exhibition of 1894. Native tribes and crafts are features of the 1923–27 and 1931–37 issues; the British explorer H. M. Stanley is shown on the series of 1928. The Congo became independent in 1960.

Formerly held by Belgium under mandate, two parts of what was German East Africa, Ruanda and Urundi, had fine pictorial stamps. Rwanda and Burundi are now separate republics with their own issues.

The philatelic story of the Grand Duchy of Luxembourg begins in 1852 with the Grand Duke William III, who was also King of Holland, but the stamps bore no name. On the death of William III the operation of the Salic law deprived Wilhelmina of the succession in Luxembourg, which went to Adolf of Nassau, and then to Grand Duke William IV. The last-named, having no male issue, took measures by statute (1907) providing for the succession of his daughter, the Grand Duchess Marie Adelaide. She succeeded in 1912, but abdicated in 1919, after which her sister, the Grand Duchess Charlotte, reigned in Luxembourg. She has been succeeded by Grand Duke Jean. The country was under German occupation, 1940–44.

Holland, or the Kingdom of the Netherlands, started in 1852 with stamps that bore the picture of King William III, with no name of the country, simply the word " Postzegel " (postage stamp). Two issues appeared before it was considered necessary to add the name Nederland. The later issues of William III and many of the Queen Wilhelmina issues present a complexity of perforation varieties, but are otherwise simple and straightforward. Later, in addition to excellent portrait engravings of the Queen, there are others of the late dowager Queen Emma and of the Crown Princess Juliana, who succeeded to the throne in 1948 upon the abdication of her mother, Queen Wilhelmina, after fifty years' rule.

The stamps of the former extensive colonial empire follow *mutatis mutandis* those of the mother country in series for the various possessions.

After the little square-type stamps of Denmark of 1851–64, all except the first showing the Danish Regalia, this country, like its Scandinavian neighbours Sweden and Norway, remained long faithful to one numeral design. It was not until 1904 that a portrait issue (King Christian IX) appeared, followed in successive reigns by pictures of Frederick VIII and Christian X, the latter of whom celebrated his silver jubilee in stamps in 1937. There was a delightful set marking the centenary of Hans Andersen's fairy tales, 1935, with Andersen, the Ugly Duckling, and the Mermaid.

The stamps of the Danish West Indies (now the Virgin Islands of the U.S.A.) and Iceland closely followed the early Danish types. Iceland in more recent times has presented some pictorial stamps, of which the most noteworthy is the series marking the millenary of the Icelandic Parliament, the Althing. Iceland was, until 1944, united with Denmark through the identity of its sovereign, who was King of both countries. The only present Danish colony is Greenland, whose first postage stamps (1938) are in two designs, one picturing the Danish King and the other the Great White Bear.

Norway's " Number One " has been much collected and studied by specialists, who have absorbed large quantities into their collections, and it is comparatively expensive in consequence. The variety showing a double foot to the lion's right leg is keenly sought after and well worth looking for.

In modern times portraits of a few celebrities, Ibsen, Björnson, Nansen, and others, have appeared on stamps, as well as views calculated to lure tourists to the fjords. Tourists flock to a little village near Trondhjem rejoicing in the name of Hell to post letters and cards to their friends from a place which holds no infernal terrors.

Sweden's first stamps in an Arms type and the old skilling-banco currency are now scarce except for the 4 sk.-bco. used. There is an error in this issue, of which only one copy is known—the 3 sk.-bco. in yellow instead of green; the stamp was sold by private treaty in 1937 for about £5,000, and was re-sold in 1953 for the record sum of £12,700.

Nevertheless, Sweden, like Denmark and Norway, has a great range of cheap and interesting varieties and some finely engraved commemoratives.

Finland, after a few issues of home manufacture, 1856–91, was then provided with stamps printed in St. Petersburg, closely resembling the contemporary Russian stamps. As pointed out in Chapter VI, little circles at the sides or in the spandrels distinguish the Finnish from the Russian types.

The modern republic has issued some pleasing commemoratives, including a short set for the centenary of the publication of the national folk poems, known as " Kalevala," and a portrait of the composer Sibelius.

Up to the close of the 1914–18 war, when independence was regained, Poland had only one postage stamp, a 10 kopecs blue and rose, similar in pattern to the contemporary Russian stamps, but inscribed " Za lot Kop 10." This was issued in 1860, and was suppressed in 1865, when Russian stamps became valid throughout a denationalised Poland. Stamps have been issued since 1918 in great variety, tracing steps in its progress; the set of 1919 marking the meeting of the Sejm or Parliament bears portraits of the late Marshal Pilsudski, and of the Premier, who was no other than that virtuoso of the piano, Paderewski. Appropriately Fredéric Chopin's portrait appeared on a stamp of 1927.

Poland was fated to undergo further subjection; first, to Nazi Germany and, after the war, to Soviet Russia. During 1941–44 the exile government in London issued stamps for use on Polish vessels and in Polish military establishments in Britain.

The republic of Czechoslovakia displayed in its recessprinted stamps a variety of beautiful scenes, as well as portraits of the late President Masaryk, and the composers Smetana and Dvořák among others. In 1929 there was an issue commemorating the millenary of the death of St. Wenceslas. Under the German occupation stamps were issued for the provinces of Bohemia and Moravia, 1939–45, and separate issues also appeared for Slovakia.

Afterward Czechoslovakia came under Soviet influence, as is readily evidenced in its stamps, which continued, however, to be beautifully produced.

In the early seventeenth century the posts in Germany and Austria were the monopoly of the princely house of Thurn and Taxis. Austria and the separate States gradually acquired, by withdrawal or purchase, their freedom from this control. In 1850 the German-Austrian Postal Union was formed to regulate interchange of mails between the Germanic States; it was joined by the Thurn and Taxis administration in 1851. By this time only a few German States were left under the Thurn and Taxis control, some in the north and others in the south, where the currencies were different. Hence the issue of two separate series of the Thurn and Taxis, one with large numerals in a square design with values in silbergroschen (30 sgr. = 1 thaler = 3s.) for the northern States; the other with the numerals in a circle for use in the southern districts is in kreuzer (60 kr. = 1 florin = 1s. 8d.).

Bavaria was the first German State to issue stamps (1849), and continued to have separate stamps until after the first World War. The only other German State retaining its separate stamps (with the exception of Austria) after the formation of the German Empire was Württemberg, which continued to 1902.

The stamps of the old German States form a grand series for collecting and study, and in fine condition are much sought after by the philatelic connoisseur. The story of the merging of these States, first into the North German Confederation (1866), and the greater merging into the Empire, is told in the disappearance of separate issues for Baden, Bavaria, Bergedorf, Bremen, Brunswick, Hamburg, Hanover, Lübeck, Mecklenburg-Schwerin, Mecklenburg-Strelitz, Oldenburg, Prussia, Saxony, Schleswig-Holstein, and the last relics of the Thurn and Taxis postal monopoly.

The makeshift stamps of 1870 generally associated with Alsace-Lorraine were used in many parts of northern France in German occupation during the Franco-Prussian war of 1870. They were hurriedly made in a type-set design printed in colour on a network ground of the same colour. The plates which printed this network in colour were the same as those used for printing an invisible protective underprint for the stamps of the North German Confederation.

The eagle displayed is the chief feature of the earliest German Empire issues, giving way to the armed figure of Germania in 1900.

The inflation period of 1923 produced an amazing race between the stamp printers and the disappearing mark. The stamp denominations in ordinary use were no longer in pfennigs, but marks; then successively in hundreds, thousands, millions, and finally milliards of marks.

More recent issues covered a wide range of subjects, some of the portraits including Schiller, Daimler, the motor-car pioneer, and Hitler. The many beautiful examples of stamp production during the Nazi régime included some depicting beauty-spots of the Fatherland.

After the end of the war Germany's philatelic history became very complicated, stamps arriving in profusion from the various Allied zones of occupation and West Berlin.

In the former German Colonies overprinted German stamps were used until 1900, when two key-plate designs showing the Kaiser's yacht *Hohenzollern* were brought into use, the colony's name being added on the duty plate.

The early stamps of Austria bear the Arms and, later, portraits of the Emperor Francis Joseph came in two different currencies. The stamps in kreuzer values were for Austria-Hungary, while those in centes(imi) were used in Lombardy-Venetia (Austrian Italy). Later soldi replaced the centesimi for Lombardy-Venetia, and for a time these were also used for Austrian post offices in Turkey, which afterwards bore the Turkish currency of paras and piastres.

At the beginning of the twentieth century the Austrian stamps were provided with an underprint of colourless but shiny bars (*celluloidlackstreifen*), which renders the stamps unsafe to immerse in water.

From 1908 the Austrian stamps have presented a wonderful picture gallery of miniature engravings of portraits and scenes. The combination of Kolomon Moser as designer, Ferdinand Schirnböck, the one-eyed master engraver, and the workmanship of the Austrian State Printing Works in Vienna gave us some of the most beautiful series of stamps in the Emperor's sixtieth anniversary of accession (1908) and eightieth birthday, 1910. The same combination had produced the fine scenic stamps of Bosnia-Herzegovina in 1906.

Many of the later issues followed worthily on the Moser-Schirnböck lines, but one stamp of 1934 produced a strange freak in a portrait of a peasant of Lower Austria, showing his ears reversed. This 6 groschen blue of 1934 was re-engraved correctly and reissued in 1935.

The Austrian stamps were used in Hungary until 1871, when separate stamps were issued with a small head of the King, first in a lithographed set, and later engraved. There followed the long-familiar design bearing a numeral of value set upon the back of an envelope. These and many subsequent issues exhibit the crown of St. Stephen with its cross at the top lop-sided. After the first World War, the Bolshevist régime under Bela Kun issued in 1920 a bizarre set of portrait stamps, including Marx and Engels. Only a week after the celebrated football victory over Britain in 1953, Hungary had stamps on sale with the score, 6–3.

Italy, like Germany, presents another instance of the

merging of many old States into one united kingdom, formerly with a colonial empire. As with Germany, the stamps
of the old States, Modena, Naples, the Neapolitan States,
Parma, Romagna, Roman States (or States of the Church),
Sardinia, Sicily, and Tuscany, are the favourites of the
connoisseurs.

Modern Italy has produced many remarkable stamps
dipping into ancient history with reference to Augustus
the Great and Julius Cæsar, into literature with Virgil,
Horace, Dante, Mazzini, Manzoni, Boccaccio, Petrarch,
Ariosto, etc. Into science also (Leonardo da Vinci, Volta,
Pacinotti, Galvani, Galileo, Marconi) and music (Bellini,
showing his fingering at the piano, Stradivari, etc.) (See
Plates 17 and 26).

Under an earlier régime the See and Church of Rome
had independent postage stamps (1852–70) for the States
under pontifical rule; they bore the device of the Papal
tiara and the crossed keys without other indication of the
country of origin. The tiara and keys reappear on the
modern issues under the restored temporal sovereignty of
the Holy See, known as the stamps of Vatican City. An
aerial view is seen on the 2 lire and the 2l. 50c. express-
delivery stamps of 1933.

The post-war disputes over Fiume led to stamp issues by
the Southern Slavs, and by Gabriele d'Annunzio's filibuster-
ing supporters. The poet's head on the issue of 1920 is one
of the most striking of stamp portraits, and his use of the
classic motto *Hic manebimus optime* (Here I am and here I stay)
was made to good purpose, for Fiume was annexed to Italy
in 1924, though it was ceded to Jugoslavia in 1947.

The little republic of San Marino, comprising a small
country on a large hill, vaunts its long-lived independence
on stamps of many issues since 1877.

The Greek stamps from 1861 and for twenty-five years

afterwards bore a large head of Hermes in a frame modelled on that of the first stamps of France. The two Olympic Games series of 1896 and 1906 contribute a selection of ancient sports. The country celebrated the Byron centenary with two stamps, one bearing a portrait of the poet, and the other the scene of his death at Missolonghi. Other pictorial issues show pictures of the glories that were, and some that are, Greece.

A group of four great rarities issued in Moldavia form the prelude to the stamps of the principality, afterwards kingdom of Roumania. These circular hand-struck stamps showing a bull's head with star between its horns and a ringed posthorn with denomination below the mouth are among the rarest of all European stamps apart from a few famous errors.

One of the most popular of later issues was that bearing the head of the young King Michael, 1928, who was succeeded by his father, King Carol II, in 1930, to return to the throne later and again be deposed at the end of 1947 when Roumania became a republic.

The stamps of Serbia, with few exceptions, are within the means of most collectors, and include the Coronation issue of 1904, the para values of which have achieved renown as the " death mask " stamps, and the stamps of 1915 showing King Peter I with some of his staff watching a battle late in 1914.

The disruption of the Austro-Hungarian Empire at the close of the 1914–18 war brought about the brief provisional stamps of Croatia (Hrvatska), the various " S.H.S." (Serbs, Croats, and Slovenes) overprints on stamps of Hungary and Bosnia, and the " chainbreaker " stamps so expressive of new-found freedom from a foreign yoke, which preface the regular stamps of the Kingdom of the Serbs, Croats, and Slovenes, now known as Jugoslavia, and which includes the old Montenegro. The old King Peter whom we saw on the battlefield stamps of 1915 and who appears on some of the S.H.S. stamps died in 1921. His son, Alexander, who succeeded him became the first King of Jugoslavia; he was assassinated at Marseilles, October 9th, 1934, when his portrait stamps were given a mourning border of black. His son, the young Peter II, and his brothers Prince Tomislav and Prince Andrey were pictured on stamps, but from 1941–45 no stamps were issued except by the exile government. During this period, however, a considerable number of stamps appeared for Croatia, which ceased to be a separate entity when the independence of Jugoslavia was restored. A republic was proclaimed in 1945.

Bulgaria's " lion " stamps of the early period bear evidence of their Russian inspiration and manufacture. A curious set in 1896 marked the baptism of Prince Boris, who became King Boris in October 1918 on the abdication of his father, " Foxy " Ferdinand. After King Boris' death, his successor, Simeon II, reigned for only three years before a republic was declared, and since then a considerable number of stamps have arrived showing the Soviet influence.

Albania's first stamps were Turkish stamps overprinted with the Albanian eagle device and the name " Shqipenia." In 1914 a well-printed set appeared with a profile of the national hero, Skanderbeg. Afterwards the portrait of the President, later King Zog, appeared on numerous stamps, as did that of King Victor Emmanuel during the Italian occupation, 1939–43.

Turkey issued stamps in 1863, and most issues up to the collapse of the old Ottoman Empire bear either the tughra (pronounced tura) or the crescent with five-pointed star, or both. These are shown among the emblems in Chapter V. The tughra is akin to our royal cypher, and was changed for each Sultan's reign. The absence of portraits or views up to 1913 is attributed to the orthodox reading of a passage in the Koran enjoining on believers the avoidance of " wine and games of chance and statues."

It was the advent of the young Turks that brought pictorial stamps to Turkey, and the post-war régime of the republic under the presidency of Kemâl Atatürk brought an abundance of pictorial issues. His portrait appears upon many of them. Just before his death in 1938 the Ghazi was shown on a series of stamps standing before a blackboard and personally teaching his followers the Latin alphabet he had introduced into Turkey ten years previously.

Under the Tsars, Russia built up what became the world's finest Government printing office for all papers of State, including the manufacture of the Russian stamps. It formed a model town complete in itself at St. Petersburg. So we find the stamps of the Imperial régime, although most of them are typographed, very attractive in their delicacy of colouring. They bear the Imperial arms on a mantle or within a crowned oval. Below the arms are two linked posthorns, to which were added in 1889 two crossed " thunderbolts " to denote the telegraph service. It was not until 1913 that the Tsars were pictured on stamps. In that year of the tercentenary of the Romanov Dynasty, Tsar Nicholas II, his predecessors, and views of his palaces appeared on a great series known as the Romanov issue.

The tercentenary of the Romanovs was near the end of their rule in Russia. In the revolution of 1917 Alexander Kerensky had stamps prepared in a design depicting a strong hand cutting with a sword the chains of servitude. Before these were issued, Kerensky's provisional Government had been superseded by the Bolshevists.

Soviet Russia has looked upon its postage stamps largely as a means of spreading its propaganda. Among its heroes we find stamp portraits of Lenin as child and man, Karl Marx, and Engels. Heroes of peaceful achievement also appear in Dr. Zamenhof (Esperantist), Maxim Gorki, Tolstoy, Pushkin, and Tschaikovsky.

Most of the countries that have come under the influence of Russia in the Union of Soviet Socialist Republics, and some of which have or had their own stamps, exhibit the symbol of the " workers of the world "—the hammer and sickle. These include countries in European Russia, in Trans-Caucasia, and beyond the far steppes of Siberia. In the Caucasus, Armenia, Azerbaijan, Batum, and Georgia had separate stamp issues for a short period after the first World War.

Estonia, Latvia and Lithuania only started issuing stamps in 1918, but each provided a considerable variety afterwards. Latvia, for want of more suitable paper, printed its first stamps on the back of German ordnance maps, and later on exercise book, cigarette and bank-note paper. Lithuania in 1919 printed stamps on paper originally made for bread-rationing tickets during the war. All three countries were incorporated into the Soviet Union some twenty years later.

Danzig ceased issuing stamps about the same time. As a Free City, it had given its stamp designs a consistent baroque character in keeping with its Hanseatic history. The German philosopher, Schopenhauer, was born in Danzig, and is pictured on three stamps of 1938, commemorating the 150th anniversary of his birth.

CHAPTER XII

SOME EASTERN LANDS
Plate 20

EGYPT WAS PART OF the Ottoman Empire when her first
stamps appeared on January 1st, 1866, in quaint arabesque
designs in colour with a black overprint in Turkish characters. In 1867 the pyramid of Cheops and the Sphinx
figured on stamps in a frame showing Pompey's Pillar at
left and Cleopatra's Needle at right. The Sphinx and
Pyramid are the feature of all subsequent issues to 1914,
when a variety of Egyptian scenes were introduced. As an
independent kingdom from 1922, Egypt had portraits of
King Fuad and of King Farouk, and many commemorative
stamps. Egypt later became a republic, and combined in
1958 with Syria to form the United Arab Republic. Both
still issued different stamps, but all were marked UAR.
Those of Egypt could be distinguished by the values marked
in milliemes. Syrian stamps are at present inscribed SAR
(Syrian Arab Republic).

Abyssinia, or Ethiopia, had some picturesque stamps
before the conquest by Italy. The first came in 1894 in
two designs, one showing Menelik II, then King of Kings
of Ethiopia, and the other the " Lion of the tribe of Judah."
Pictorial issues have since portrayed the old Empress
Zauditu, Ras Taffari, and a few examples of inhabitants of
the jungle—giraffes, gazelle, spotted leopard, ostriches, a
rhinoceros, buffalo, and lions. On the annexation by Italy,
1936, an Italian commemorative set, inscribed Etiopia,
appeared, but the country was afterwards served with
stamps of Italian East Africa until independence was restored.

98

Lawrence of Arabia took an active part in the preparation of the first stamps of the Hejaz, where are the holy cities of Mecca and Medina. The Grand Sherif Hussein proclaimed his country's independence during the war, in 1916, but the Islamic world was being deceived by the Turks with false news. So the main idea of providing Hussein with stamps was to confirm and disseminate the news of Arab independence in the Hejaz. The first stamps were rushed out to be ready for the pilgrim season, when countless letters were posted by the faithful back to their home countries. The designs are arabesques drawn from many Moslem sources.

Ibn Saud with his Wahabis ousted King Hussein, and added the Hejaz to his country of Nejd, since when there have been common issues in use throughout Hejaz-Nejd (later known as Saudi Arabia).

Although overrun by Ibn Saud in 1934, the kingdom of the Yemen retained its separate identity under the Treaty of Taif concluded in June 1934. Its few inland stamps with two crossed swords, issued in 1926, are crude but interesting. The later issues of 1930 and 1931 are less attractive, but better printed, being "made in Germany." Following the rebel coup of 1962, both "Republic" and "Royalist" administrations have issued their own stamps.

It is an almost incredible tale, like one of the adventures of Hajji Baba, that tells of the making of the first " lion " stamps of Iran (Persia). The clichés, four for each value, made from original dies engraved by Albert Barre in Paris, were sent to Teheran about 1865, and in true Oriental fashion were allowed to lie there. In 1868 Shah Nasr-ed-Din bethought himself of Persia's need of stamps; the copper electros were found, and handed over to a cook who could turn his hand to anything. The Persian idea of printing was first to rub ink on the face of the clichés, lay a small piece of paper over it, and press on top with the palm of the hand.

Hence the crude impressions which the Shah scattered so indiscriminately that they were of little use for collecting postage.

A postal officer of experience was lent from Austria to Teheran to place the Persian postal service on sound lines, and in 1876 the first Viennese portrait stamps of Nasr-ed-Din appeared. These were followed by a long succession of fine portrait stamps of the Shahs, whose religion (the Shiah sect) did not forbid them to represent pictures, as did the Suni persuasion of the Turks.

The portraits of all the Shahs from Nasr-ed-Din to Ahmed appear on the stamps, and the Ahmed coronation issue presents King Darius on his throne, and the gateway of the Palace of Persepolis (1915).

The rise of Riza Khan Pahlavi brought many stamps with his picture, as Shah, including a set showing his enthronement on the throne of Darius, 1929. The change of name from Persia to Iran was denoted on the stamps in 1935.

Afghanistan did not become a member of the Universal Postal Union until April 1st, 1928, but it has had stamps for internal postage from 1870. Inscribed in native characters, the early issues, circular in design, have a face in the centre, which is intended to represent a lion. Later issues in rectangular form show a crude device of a mosque, with flags and crossed cannon (1893 onwards), and as an Islamic country we note the use of the crescent and the tughra. Since King Amanullah attempted, with little success, the Westernisation of his country in emulation of Kemâl Atatürk's reforms in Turkey, the Afghanistan stamps have been given a more pictorial aspect and some inscription in Latin characters.

The independent kingdom of Nepal, home of the Gurkhas in the Himalayas, has had native-made stamps on native paper for its earlier issues. From 1907 the Nepalese stamps showed the god Siva, the Destroyer, but latterly there have been other pictorial stamps.

Bordering on Nepal is another land which long guarded its secrets from the white man—Tibet. The native-made stamps picture the white lion in two designs of 1912 and 1933. For a brief period from 1911 Chinese stamps were overprinted for use in Chinese post offices there, with Chinese inscriptions, but the values are expressed in Indian currency—pies, annas, rupees.

Burma, separated from India in 1937, was soon issuing stamps of its own, bearing, in association with the royal profile, pictorial subjects, including the royal barge, elephants logging Burma teak, a scene on the Irrawaddy, a peacock, and a shrine. During the Japanese occupation, 1942–45, there was a wide variety of peacock overprints, followed by definitive issues. Burma became completely independent in 1948.

Siam (Thailand) issued stamps in 1883 bearing line-engraved profiles of King Chulalongkorn. From 1887–99 the stamps are typographed, and the portraits full-face. The philatelic story of this country is largely made up of a great variety of surcharged provisionals. The last stamps of the reign (1910) show the Krut, half-man, half-bird, said to correspond with the Garuda of Hindu mythology, which is the Siamese emblem of the air mail, seen in flight on the air stamps of 1925 onwards.

The stamps of China abound in designs representing ancient and mythical lore. They start with the Imperial dragon (1878 and 1885 issues), whose anatomy is peculiar. As an Imperial emblem it has five claws to each foot. As with the sixteen-petalled chrysanthemum in Japan, no one was permitted, under dire penalties, to use the emblem with five claws. Apart from these extremities, the beast has the head of a camel, horns of a deer, eyes of a rabbit, ears of a cow, neck of a snake, belly of a frog, scales of a carp, claws of a hawk, and palms of a tiger. On the stamps it is seen guarding the night-shining pearl.

All the stamps of the old Empire follow in much the same key—not only the central designs, but every attribute or detail in the frames has its foundations in Chinese philosophy and geomancy.

Since China became a republic her stamps are Western-ised so far as the quality of manufacture is concerned, but retain the elaborate symbolism of the East in their designs. For many years Dr. Sun Yat Sen was a popular subject, but following the establishment of the Chinese People's Republic in 1949 first regional and then general issues appeared bearing traces of Soviet influence. The war with Japan and the civil war had meantime left a substantial legacy of overprints and special issues. Some modern stamps of China overprinted in Chinese were thus marked for use in provinces where the currency varied. In recent years stamps have been issued for Formosa, many of them bearing portraits of Chiang Kai-shek.

Following the foundation under Japanese influence of the state of Manchuria, separate stamps were issued. Designs of 1932 were shared between the Liaoyang pagoda and the spectacled Mr. Pu Yi, afterwards the Emperor Kangteh. After his coronation in 1934, Manchurian stamps bore the orchid (see page 30) as the Imperial crest. Manchuria has, however, been a part of China since 1945, and rival issues appeared for a time from the Chiang Kai Shek administration and the People's Government.

The former independent kingdom of Korea had prepared in 1885 to issue stamps bearing the yin-yang symbol in the centre. The Koreans were not ready for such a Western reform: they set fire to the post office and killed a few officials, including the postmaster. Only two values out of five were ever used, and those are well-nigh unobtainable in the used condition. All five are cheap unused.

Ten years elapsed before Korea got a proper start, in 1895. The yin-yang reappears in a different form, but the Imperial crest indicating the Emperor's sanction is shown on all Korean stamps except the abortive issue of 1885. This crest is a five-petalled cherry blossom, shown among the Oriental symbols on page 29.

Other designs include the Imperial cap, or "Ming bonnet," of 1902, and the Imperial falcon with the yin-yang on its breast in 1903. In 1905 Japan took over the Korean posts, and in 1910 Korea was merged in the Empire of Japan. Korea revived as a stamp-issuing country in 1946 under Allied occupation, and from 1948 both South Korea and North Korea had stamps.

The stamps of Japan are in designs and subjects even more rich in Oriental inspiration than those of China. Over a hundred designs link ancient mythological subjects with modern achievements. With few exceptions they have been the work of Japanese artists, engravers, and printers. In the years since 1938 many lovely photogravure stamps have appeared depicting the natural beauties of Japan. Except for the first or "dragon" type stamps of 1871–72, the chrysanthemum crest appeared in all issues right up to May 1947.

The peak season in the Japanese posts is New Year, when it is customary to send greetings. In an effort like our post office's "post early for Christmas," Japan in 1935 and the two following years issued special New Year stamps, so that greetings could be posted during several weeks before, to be held at post offices of destination for delivery on New Year's Day.

CHAPTER XIII

UNITED STATES OF AMERICA— CONFEDERATE STATES — HAWAIIAN ISLANDS

Plates 21 and 22

EACH COUNTRY HAD ITS own problems in achieving postage reforms comparable to those introduced in Great Britain in 1840. To begin with, a uniform inland postage rate presented vast difficulties in a great country like the United States. A limited measure of uniformity was established in 1845, allowing a ½-oz. letter at 5 cents over a distance not exceeding 300 miles. At that time no stamps were provided, and prepayment of postage was not obligatory. Between 1845 and 1847 a few postmasters, knowing their remuneration to be dependent upon postages collected, had the enterprise to provide stamps to encourage prepayment at their offices.

The postmasters' provisional stamps of that period are of historic interest, and some are of great rarity. In some cases they were adhesive stamps, in others stamped envelopes. Only the New York stamp, 5 cents black, ever was comparatively plentiful. The latter is a beautiful Washington head, fit to take its place as America's " penny black."

In 1847 the Government suppressed the postmasters' stamps and issued the first regular postage stamps of the U.S.A., 5 cents brown (Franklin) and 10 cents black (Washington). The issue began on July 1st, but as the prepayment of postage was neither compulsory nor customary, their use was far from general. In the four years they were in circulation fewer than 4,000,000 of the 5 cents and only about 800,000 of the 10 cents were sold.

The simple dignity of their portraiture and design and the excellence of their line-engraving set a standard which successive private contractors maintained remarkably well during nearly half a century. The stamps of the United States are nearly all line-engraved, and the designs have been based upon portraiture of great citizens of the Republic throughout its history. No President, statesman, or hero has been admitted to the nation's postage-stamp gallery during his lifetime. You may read from the long sequence of portraits much of the history of the growth of the nation. George Washington, as the Father of his country, is rarely absent from any portrait series, and Benjamin Franklin is almost equally familiar on the stamps throughout. Franklin, in addition to his other distinguished services, was the most notable figure in American postal history. For many years he was postmaster of Philadelphia and a joint Postmaster-General for America.

In 1851 a new issue began to appear; it developed a wider range of denominations, 1 cent to 90 cents, and all charming in engraving and colour. The frames were more elaborate, but well subordinated to the central portraits, which are all of Franklin and Washington, except the 5 cents brown, which has a three-quarters-face picture of Thomas Jefferson, in what one may call a bank-note frame.

Perforation of U.S. stamps began in 1857, the gauge being 15, but with a new issue started in 1861 the perforation measured 12. Perf. 12 is the standard gauge met with on U.S. stamps for the next fifty years, 1861-1914.

The stamps of the 1851-60 designs were still current when the Civil War broke out, and eleven of the States seceded from the Union, setting up an independent Government, the Confederate States of America. The post offices in the seceded States held stocks of the contemporary United States stamps, and it became necessary for the Union to issue a new series, and later to demonetise the stamps of 1847 and 1851-60.

The new stamps began to appear in August 1861, another beautiful set, but some of the denominations admitted of slight improvements, which were duly effected on the dies. The revised and full series followed almost immediately, and although the two groups are commonly spoken of as the August and September issues, the 1, 3, 5, and 10 cents of the improved types were in circulation before the end of August.

Stamps of the first designs, distinguished as *premières gravures*, are rare, but the differences are so slight that many a collector has found the rare type (especially of the 10 cents green) among the commoner stamps of the definitive issue.

Two new denominations added in 1863 and 1866 call for special attention. The first was a 2 cents black, needed to prepay the minimum rate for " drop letters "; that is to say, letters deposited for local delivery: the rate had been reduced from 3 cents for this service. The design, nearly all head, pictures Andrew Jackson. Collectors in England used to call it the " Big head," but it is now best known by the American nickname of " Black Jack."

The registration fee was fixed at 15 cents in 1866, so a stamp of this denomination was issued. The previous year Abraham Lincoln had been slain by an assassin; the nation was still mourning the tragic end of her noble orator and great statesman. It was not, however, as a " mourning " stamp that Lincoln's portrait was used on the new 15 cents stamp, although it was appropriately printed in black.

As in Great Britain, so in the United States there was constant scheming to make it impossible to clean the cancellations off stamps to use them over again. About this period and during the currency of the next two issues the stamps are met with having a roughening of their surface caused by a *grille*. This was a device designed to break into the fibres of the paper after the stamps had been printed, so that the ink of the postmark would saturate into the paper fibres. The grille was effected very simply by passing a roller with small pyramidal bosses over the stamp sheet which had been laid upon a sheet of lead.

The grille does not improve the appearance of the stamps (see Plate 28, Stamp 10), but often enhances the catalogue price. One or two stamps " grilled all over " are of great rarity, but the grilles being easily and commonly faked, they should be left to the specialist.

The little square stamps of 1869 brought the first attempt at pictorial variety into the stamps. They bear three portraits: Franklin on the 1 cent, Washington on the 2 cents, and Lincoln on the bicoloured 90 cents. Interspersed with these are: 2 cents an express rider, 3 cents a locomotive, 10 cents and 30 cents heraldic shield, 12 cents a mail steamer, 15 cents the landing of Columbus, 24 cents the Declaration of Independence. The last two are little miracles of microscopic engraving, taken from large historical paintings. In 1870 there was a return to the good and large style of portrait stamps, and nearly all from sculptured busts.

In 1892, when John Wanamaker (of " Stores " fame) was Postmaster-General, he put over a big idea to advertise the Chicago World Fair, celebrate the four hundredth anniversary of the discovery of America by Columbus, and to show how stamp collectors might be persuaded to help reduce the deficit on the Post Office Department. The series of sixteen stamps of large size, in denominations from 1 cent to $5, is a very fine one, well engraved with diversified scenes drawn from paintings and bronzes illustrating the story of Columbus. The subjects do not follow in chronological sequence, and one does not look to them for exact historical detail. It was early noted that on the 1 cent blue " Columbus in sight of land " was smooth of chin, but on the 2 cents purple " Landing of Columbus " (time, a few hours later) he is decorated with a full beard.

A neat style of portrait stamps approximately the same size as the British stamps was current from 1890 until the important change which gave the printing of all U.S. postage stamps to the Bureau of Engraving and Printing, which is a Department of the Treasury at Washington entrusted with the manufacture of security papers of many kinds.

The Bureau is magnificently equipped, but it has not lacked the human touch that admits an occasional rare " error." Of the six bicoloured stamps of the Pan-American Exhibition series of 1901, three of the values, 1 cent, 2 cents, and 4 cents, are known with the centres inverted. The first air-mail stamp, 24 cents blue and carmine, issued in 1918, also exists with the mail plane upside down, and this is one of the great rarities among air stamps.

An unusual kind of mistake to get into actual circulation was the 5 cents Washington of 1917 printed in the carmine-rose colour of the 2 cents Washington. This is how it happened. A steel plate of 400 2 cents had been laid down in four panes of 100. On inspection of a proof-sheet, three images were found to be defective. Their positions were stamps 74 and 84 in the top left pane, and No. 18 in the lower right pane. The proof-sheet marked for correction at these points was returned to the transferer. To make the fresh entries at these points the operator inadvertently used the wrong roller die as used for the 5 cents. Thus the plate as " corrected " bore 397 2 cents plus three 5 cents images. The mistakes should have been detected before the plate was put to press, but they were not; the printed sheets (50,000 of 400) passed the inspection room, and were packed up and sealed for distribution to post offices.

No one appeared to have noticed the blunder until the post-master of a small town in Virginia wrote to the Department in Washington " not to mix the values on the same sheets, for he had quite enough trouble keeping his accounts straight."

In 1962–63 the Bureau deliberately printed 180 million Hammarskjöld " inverted yellow " errors to stop speculation.

With Mr. Franklin D. Roosevelt, a lifelong collector, as President, the stamps issued during his terms of office and since have been of great variety. It was Mr. Roosevelt who authorised the preparation and issue of the long set of 1938 presenting the complete range of deceased U.S. Presidents.

Very many attractive stamps have appeared over the years commemorating a wide variety of subjects, such as the centenary of the Pony Express, Hawaii Statehood, the centenary of the inauguration of the Atlantic Cable, and the fiftieth anniversary of Rotary International.

Apart from the general issues for the United States, there have been special stamps for newspapers and periodicals, for departmental correspondence, parcels post, special (i.e. express) delivery, registration, and postage due.

The Philatelic Agency of the Washington Post Office was set up in December 1921 to provide special service to stamp collectors and the stamp trade.

CONFEDERATE STATES.—Cut off from the postal service of the North during the Civil War, Southern postmasters showed their resourcefulness in forwarding mails and collecting postage. Many, following the early precedent of the postmasters' stamps of 1845–47, provided their own adhesive stamps or stamped envelopes. Some were editors, printers, or proprietors of local newspapers as well as postmasters, so had no difficulty in preparing temporary stamps. At Greenville, Alabama, the postmaster was a judge and an amateur printer; he printed his little labels, and would have been amazed at the prices letters bearing them have realised in salerooms.

Others, less well equipped, carved primitive stamp dies on wood or cork. At Emory, Virginia, the postmaster cut his die on the end of a piece of poplar, and for ready-made gummed paper he trimmed off the stamp edging from his useless stock of U.S. stamps: a strange freak, this rebel stamp on loyal paper.

When the Confederate States Government started to prepare regular stamps, it met with considerable difficulties. An old German lithographer drew the first stamps on stone, using a *carte de visite* of Jefferson Davis. An emissary was sent to London to arrange for supplies of stamps and plates from Messrs. de la Rue & Co. A consignment was lost when the steamship *Bermuda* was taken by the Federal fleet, but most of the stamps sent out reached Richmond.

Meanwhile a Northern engraver came to Richmond, and saw a prospect of doing good business in printing stamps and paper money. His name was John Archer, and " a well-to-do plasterer " of Richmond joined him as Archer & Daly, " Bank Note Engravers." Archer's first die of the " 10 " cents with " frame line " cracked after one small plate of 100 had been made from it.

The contractors' difficulties increased as the Confederate cause waned. Supplies failed as the blockade became more effective. A keg of rose dry colour received through the blockade and stored in the press-room for making ink was depleted by young ladies on war service and assisting in the making of stamps and paper money. They helped themselves to the colour for use as rouge.

Federal pressure on the capital made it necessary to shift the works to Columbia, South Carolina. There, along with much other material, they were destroyed in the fire which devastated the city when General Sherman captured it.

HAWAIIAN ISLANDS.—Now a territory of the United States, the old Kingdom of Hawaii issued in 1851 some primitive locally printed stamps which are now among the greatest rarities. They are popularly called " Missionaries," for collectors first got to know about them from correspondence sent home by missionaries. Later some handsome issues engraved in the U.S.A. presented a fascinating portrait gallery of the Kamehamehas and their dynasty.

CHAPTER XIV

THE OTHER AMERICAS
Plates 23 and 24

MEXICO WRITES HER CHEQUERED story on stamps, and there is variety of scene and theme to interest you in the Mexican pages of the stamp album. The curé of Dolores, the " Great Deliverer " Hidalgo, figures on the first issues of 1856 and 1864; the short-lived empire of 1864–67 changed the portrait to that of the ill-fated Emperor Maximilian of the tragic House of Hapsburg. A firing party at dawn on the Cerro de las Campanos, near Querétaro, ended Maximilian and his empire. A crude series of lithographed stamps showing Hidalgo full face in 1868 was followed in 1872 by an issue with the priest's profile turned to left. This set is peculiar in that the paper has a blue moiré pattern on the back.

All the Mexican stamps up to 1884 are found overprinted with district names, and some with dates and consignment numbers as well. These additions are part of elaborate systems of control.

It was often difficult to maintain distribution of adequate stamp supplies, and most of the higher values are met with bisected or even quartered for use as half or quarter the face value of the whole.

Among the middle issues the Hidalgos of 1884 and the numerals of 1886 are finely engraved, and printed under such pressure as to give them the effect of embossing. Later issues depict methods of postal transport, views, a gallery of heroes and some heroines, and many peeps into the ancient civilisation of the Aztecs.

Revolution has often disturbed the processes of postal service, and brought a plethora of local issues and rebel stamps, which fill many pages in the stamp catalogues.

The stamps inscribed " Porte de Mar " (i.e. sea postage) issued in 1875 were used to indicate the proportion of prepaid postage due to the shipping company for the transmission of letters to places overseas.

The Central American Republics have played a colourful part in stamps as well as in romance. All of them have at times displayed an excessive zeal in producing stamps for collectors. In the 'nineties three of these States, Honduras, Nicaragua, and Salvador, fell in with the subtle wiles of a philatelist, the late Nicholas F. Seebeck, who represented the Hamilton Bank Note Company of New York; he contracted to print their stamps free of charge on conditions briefly outlined under the term " Seebecks " in Chapter XIX.

Among collectors the opprobrium attached to the " Seebeck " countries has not been entirely dispelled; there have been epidemics of surcharging and over-production, keeping alive suspicion and disfavour among collectors.

Shorn of the superfluities, there is much of interest in the stamps of these republics. Costa Rica (" Rich Coast "), the most moderate of the group, issued her first stamps in October 1862. They show not just a painted ship upon a painted ocean, but two ships upon two oceans. The stars indicate the five provinces (now there are seven).

Costa Rican stamps sold in the province of Guanacaste between 1885 and 1889 were overprinted with the name, as they were sold at a rebate of 12 per cent. in that province, on account of currency variation. On the Costa Rican stamps of 1924 is a map of this rich province where minerals and forests abound, and lean kine bought across the border in Nicaragua are speedily turned into fat kine.

Nicaragua in 1862 displayed her mountains on the first stamps. Mr. Seebeck provided a useful map design in

1896, showing how the width of the country was broken up by great lakes, indicating its potentialities for the cutting of an Isthmian Canal. There were two rival routes, via Panama or via Nicaragua. Unfortunately for the latter, the country had shown on stamps what her volcanoes could do. Mt. Momotombo in eruption and the populace fleeing in terror to the sea provides the picture on the 1900 issue.

Nicaragua has probably produced more surcharge varieties than any other country. It reached a limit in 1911, when a stock of railway stamps, already surcharged for fiscal stamps, was again surcharged (on the backs) for postage stamps.

Guatemala got its first Arms-type stamps from France, 1871, and later there was a striking picture of the head of an Indian woman (1878). The favourites among the early issues are the bicoloured Quetzal stamps, 1879 and 1881. The sacred bird of the Mayas is in green on all of them, different colours being used for the frames. Three of the 1881 values exist as errors with the Quetzal inverted.

The bird adorns many other Guatemalan stamps, but turn for a moment to the London-printed pictorials of 1902 ; they will illustrate some of the marvels of line-engraving. On the pillared portico of the Temple of Minerva (one of the sights of the capital), read the inscription " Manuel Estrada Cabrera Presidente de la República a la Juventud Estudiosa " in one line barely half a centimetre in length.

The republic of Honduras, which is to be distinguished from our colony of British Honduras, which lies north of it, issued stamps in 1866 bearing its Arms device. The Seebeck period was cut short, 1890–95, and the stamps which followed include many interesting, if crude, local productions. The old-time American locomotive, with cow-catcher, hauling a train (1898 issue) has been a favourite with young collectors.

Stamps of El Salvador during the first twenty years

1867–87 are of considerable interest, and have been much studied by advanced collectors. The country then became the head and front of Mr. Seebeck's offending, being the first to enter into his contract and fulfilling its terms for the full ten years 1889–99. One must recognise, however, the quality of the engraving and the interest of the designs, especially those of 1892, 1893, and 1894, which supplement the postage-stamp panorama of the life of Columbus. Subsequent issues tell of revolution, but also of modern progress and sport. The industries, especially balsam, coffee, and sugar, are brought to notice on the stamps.

Panama, reminiscent of the pirate Henry Morgan and the freebooter William Parker, entered the stamp orbit in 1878, as one of the United States of Colombia. The isthmus was featured from the commencement, and the map stamps attracted world-wide attention to the exceptional position of a narrow strip of country separating two vast oceans. The State seceded from Colombia in 1903 and entered into the treaty with the United States, establishing the Canal Zone. From 1904 onwards we find on the stamps of the republic and the stamps of the Canal Zone Administration (now discontinued) a fascinating record of the great achievement.

The South American Republics are all large countries in the philatelic as well as in the geographical sense. Here it will be possible to give only a few indications of their relative interest to collectors.

Brazil, as the first big country to follow Britain's example in issuing stamps, July 1st, 1843, produced the large numeral stamps which collectors call " bull's-eyes." It had been the intention to follow the British stamps in presenting the Emperor's head, but a zealous official deemed that unwise, as the head of majesty was not a suitable subject for cancellation. The Dom Pedro issues which followed in 1866 are among the most handsome of portrait stamps. The constellation of the Southern Cross and the Sugar Loaf Mountain are standard features of the middle issues. In modern times Brazil has issued numerous commemoratives. Among the " Officials " we get a real high denomination of 1,000,000 reis black and sepia, issued in 1913.

Several provinces of the Argentine Republic had stamps before the general issues. There were Buenos Aires ships (barquitos), 1858; Cordoba, 1858; and Corrientes, 1856. The Corrientes stamps were engraved eight times on a copper plate by a baker's boy, who was given an early French stamp to follow as his model.

The great period of the Argentine stamps proper was from 1864, with its Rivadavia portraits and the grand range of portraiture that followed on the stamps of the subsequent fifty years.

Bolivia and Paraguay are both of slighter importance in philately than their larger neighbours. In their long-protracted war for the Gran Chaco, each of these countries presented its claims on stamps in map form.

The first Chilean stamps came from the same atelier as our early British line-engraved stamps. The name Colon on them is the Spanish form of the name Columbus, of whom we get a number of different portraits on later issues. Nearly all this country's issues are fine productions, and latterly have followed the trend of using stamps for propaganda of industries. A mechanical shovel does not commend itself as an effective subject for a stamp design, but one of those modern monsters is seen on the 10 pesos of 1936.

Ecuador was one of the " Seebeck " countries (1892–96), but apart from that and a few more blots on its philatelic escutcheon, it has a few issues of interest. The triumph of the " Liberal Party " at the elections of 1895 is celebrated in a set of curious large stamps of 1896. In 1936 we meet

Charles Darwin's portrait and the *Beagle* in a series marking the centenary of the great naturalist's visit to the Galapagos Islands.

Peru borrowed her first stamps from the Pacific Steam Navigation Company, and examples of the ship stamps genuinely used from Lima or Callao are rare. The llama figures in the Arms and on a number of the early Peruvian stamps, including the wild vicuña species (1866). There is a good deal of history written in stamp and surcharge, and Chilean stamps used in Peru during the war of 1881–83 are much sought after, being recognisable by bearing postmarks of Peruvian towns.

The Granada Confederation and the United States of New Granada are the names recorded on the earliest stamps of Colombia (1858–61). From 1862 they bear the style United States of Colombia, and from the new Constitution of 1886 Republic of Colombia. All the early stamps were of local lithographic production, and provide an almost inexhaustible field for study.

The general collector should not neglect them, or the separate issues for the numerous States, Antioquia, Bolivar, Boyaca, Cundinamarca, Santander, and Tolima. Panama (a former member of the Colombian group) seceded in 1903, and her stamps are referred to above. Ecuador and Venezuela also had been members of the old Confederation, but seceded in 1830.

Separate issues for the States, which had been necessary owing to currency variations, ceased on the passing of the Money Law of 1907. Since then there is but one stamp-issuing Colombia, whose stamps were in many instances rather poorer lithographs than the very early issues. There have also been some fine pictorials, engraved and printed abroad, illustrating the vast resources in minerals, oil, and especially emeralds, of which last Colombia has the only producing mines in the world. A fine specimen of a gleaming emerald is depicted on 3 pesos and 5 pesos stamps of 1932.

Uruguay's first stamps, known as the " Diligencias," 1856–57, were a private enterprise of the contractor who ran the postal diligences. Montevideo (" I see a mountain "), the capital, gives its name to the square issues up to 1862, and thereafter stamps of W. H. Hudson's " Purple Land that England lost " is known as the República Oriental del Uruguay. More than a hundred distinct issues have appeared, presenting allegories, portraits, views, and historical episodes.

Venezuela features the Liberator Simon Bolivar on her stamps. His funeral is depicted on a stamp of 1942. The boundary dispute with Great Britain led to the issue of map stamps (1896) in which the republic's claim was staked out. It was settled by arbitration in 1899. In that year and for several years after the country was in a continuous state of revolution, causing many rebel issues of stamps.

The republics of Santo Domingo and Haiti share the second largest island of the Greater Antilles. The Dominican Republic has had stamps from 1865, neat little typographed stamps of rare interest. In 1900 a map of the island on the stamps caused friction with the neighbouring republic of Haiti, but many years after both States issued stamps celebrating the frontier agreement. Haiti was much later in providing its own postal facilities, but it had a native sculptor to design the first Liberty head issues, 1881–87. The stirring history of the island in the times of Toussaint l'Ouverture and J. J. Dessalines is recalled by Haitian stamps, which also pay tribute to literature by representing three generations of the Dumas family on stamps of 1935.

The stamps of Cuba and Porto Rico afford historical links between the New and the Old Worlds. There is the family likeness to the stamps of Spain in the earliest issues in the old real currency, " real plata fuerta " coined silver money, later changed to centimos of a peseta. At first the two colonies shared the same stamps, but after 1873 they had separate issues, except that for a year or two Porto Rico stamps were borrowed from Cuba and overprinted with paraphs. The Spanish-American War brought both islands under United States protection, bringing overprinted U.S. stamps into use, and last of all giving Cuba its own stamps as an independent republic, 1902, and abolishing separate stamps for Puerto Rico, which now uses ordinary U.S. stamps without overprint. The U.S. Congress restored the Spanish name " Puerto Rico " by an Act of 1932. Cuba was one of the several American republics commemorating the centenary of penny postage by an issue with a portrait of Rowland Hill.

PLATE 1.—PIONEER STAMPS, 1840–49

Great Britain 1845: 1d. black, 2d. blue, 1d. black lettered V–R at top. Zürich, Geneva 1843.
Basle 1845. Mauritius 1847. Brazil 1843. United States 1847. Belgium, France, Bavaria
1849.

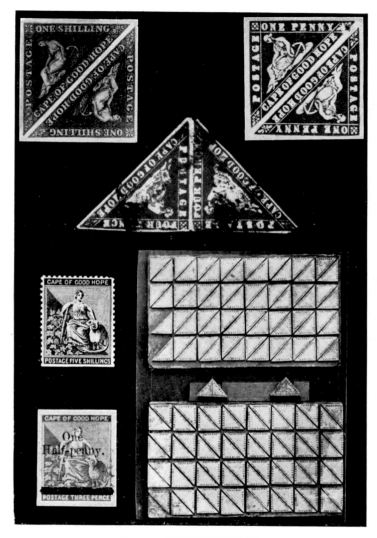

PLATE 2.—CAPE OF GOOD HOPE

1. The finely engraved London-printed triangulars. 2. Provisional printing from stereotypes in Cape Town. 3. Pair of the 4*d.* provisionals *tête-bêche*. Although commonly called "wood-blocks," the dies were engraved in relief on steel; the original mounted stereotypes are still preserved (defaced) in the Cape Town Museum, as shown in the reduced-size photographs. At left the rectangular 5*s.*; and provisional surcharge of 1882.

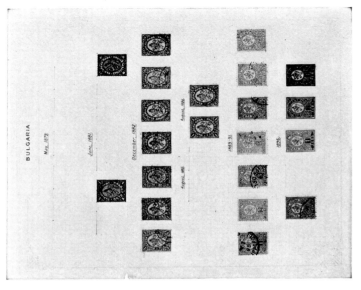

PLATE 3.—ARRANGEMENT AND WRITING-UP
Austria and Bulgaria. See page 26.

PLATE 4.—ERRORS

1. British Guiana, Patimus for Petimus. 2. Mauritius, Penoe for Pence. 3. Sweden, 20 in figures, tretio (thirty) öre in words. 4. Modena, N of cent sideways. 5 and 6. France, Descartes' book mistitled and corrected. 7 and 8. Greece, Sir Codrington, corrected to Sir Edward Codrington. 9. Lord Bacon (for Lord Verulam). 10 and 11. Inverted centres. Tonga and Guatemala. 12. Philippine Islands, the wrong scene.

PLATE 5.—GREAT BRITAIN

Line engraved, 1840–1880. Stars in upper corners: 1d. black, 2d. blue, 2d. blue with white lines, 2d. perforated. Check letters in all four corners: 1½d. rose-red, ½d. rose-red, 1½d. error of lettering OP–PC for CP–PC. 1d. rose plate number 225 on each stamp, in circle on margin, and showing current number 268. Embossed adhesives, 1847–54: 1s., 10d., and 6d.

PLATE 6.—GREAT BRITAIN

Queen Elizabeth issues. No. 1. Jersey, and: 3. Isle of Man "Regionals"; 2. Coronation; 4. Lawrence painting, "Master Lambton"; 5. Post Office Tower; 6. Christmas, Murillo's "Madonna and Child"; 7. Shakespeare; 8. Churchill; 9. Old, and: 11. new definitives; 10. Chichester's "Gipsy Moth IV".

PLATE 7.—BRITISH COMMONWEALTH
XIX Century. North America.

PLATE 8.—BRITISH COMMONWEALTH
XIX Century. Asia.

PLATE 9.—BRITISH COMMONWEALTH
XIX Century. Australasia.

PLATE 10.—BRITISH COMMONWEALTH
King George VI and Queen Elizabeth II. West Indies

PLATE 11.—FRANCE AND FRENCH COLONIES

France. 1 and 2. Modern issues; 3. Ceres; 4 and 5. Louis Napoleon as President and Emperor;
6. Crowned with laurel; 7 and 8. Reunion; 9. New Caledonia; 10. Colonial keyplate,
Commerce and Navigation; 11. Gaboon; 12. Annam; 13. Cambodia.

PLATE 12
1–4. Portugal and Colonies. 5, 6. Belgium. 7. Belgian Congo. 8. Luxembourg. 9–11. Holland.
12. Denmark. 13. Iceland. 14. Greenland.

PLATE 13

1. Sweden. 2. Norway. 3. Finland. 4. Estonia. 5. Latvia. 6. Lithuania. 7. Danzig. 8–10. Poland. 11, 12. Czechoslovakia. 13. Slovakia.

PLATE 14.—OLD GERMANY

Baden. Bavaria. Bergedorf. Bremen. Brunswick. Hamburg. Hanover. Mecklenburg-Schwerin. Lübeck. Oldenburg. Prussia. Saxony. Schleswig-Holstein. Thurn and Taxis. Württemberg.

PLATE 15.—MODERN GERMANY

1. "Inflation" stamp; 2. Hindenburg; 3. "Swastika" official. West Germany — 4. Numeral definitive; 5. Thomas Mann; 6. Hamburg Stamp Centenary; 7. Schumann. East Germany — 8. Berlin Zoo; 9. Train ferry, German Railways. West Berlin — 10. "Stamp day"; 11. President Lübke; 12. German eagle.

PLATE 16

1. Austria. 2. Hungary. 3, 4 and 5. Greece. 6, 7. Roumania. 8. Serbia. 9, 10. Jugoslavia.

PLATE 17.—MODERN ITALY

1. Michelangelo's "Jonah", and: 3. "Ezekiel"; 2. Tourist Year; 4. Air stamp; 5. Postal Conference, Paris; 6. "The Discus Thrower"; 7. Caravaggio (self-portrait); 8. Leoncavallo's Prologue to "I Pagliacci"; 9. San Marino; 10. Vatican City.

PLATE 18
1, 2. Bulgaria. 3, 4. Albania. 5–9. Turkey

PLATE 19

1, 2 and 3. Imperial Russia. 4. Kerensky regime. 5–8. Soviet Russia. 9. Armenia. 10. Azerbaidjan. 11. Ukraine.

PLATE 20.—CHINA AND JAPAN

PLATE 21.—UNITED STATES OF AMERICA
XIX Century issues.

PLATE 22.—MODERN UNITED STATES

1. The Alamo; 2. U.S. Flag; 3. Air stamp; 4. Theodore Roosevelt; 5. Pony Express;
6. George C. Marshall; 7. Appomattox; 8. "Freedom of the Press"; 9. Sam Houston;
10. Louisiana—Mississippi river-boat; 11. Davy Crockett.

PLATE 23.—MEXICO AND CENTRAL AMERICA
1, 2 and 3. Mexico. 4, 5. Honduras. 6. Salvador. 7. Nicaragua. 8, 9. Costa Rica.

PLATE 24.—SOUTH AMERICA
1. Chile. 2. Venezuela. 3, 4. Brazil. 5. Paraguay. 6, 7. Argentina. 8. Colombia. 9. Uruguay.
10. Peru. 11. Bolivia. 12. Ecuador.

PLATE 25.—AT THE STAMP ZOO

1. Platypus. 2. Hornbill. 3. Ant-eater. 4. Lyre bird. 5. Koala. 6. Kangaroo. 7. Kookaburra.
8. Kea and Kaka. 9. Okapi. 10. Kiwi. 11. Malayan stag. 12. Proboscis Monkey. 13. Argus
Pheasant.

PLATE 26.—THERE'S MUSIC IN STAMPS

1. Mozart. 2. Bach. 3. Beethoven. 4. Handel. 5. Stradivari. 6. Chopin. 7. Beethoven.
8. Paderewski. 9. Dvořák. 10. An excerpt from an opera. 11. The fingering of Vincent
Bellini.

PLATE 27.—PHILATELIC TERMS

1. Barred. 2, 3. Bisects. 4. Cancelled to order. 5. Carriers'. 6. Centred. 7. Off centre. 8. Cracked plate. 9. Control. 10. Control with Jubilee Line. 11. Control with date. 12. Current number. 13. Control and Cylinder number. 14. French Control.

PLATE 28.—PHILATELIC TERMS

1. Cubierta. 2. Cut square. 3. Cut to shape. 4. Dominical label. 5. Encased. 6, 7. Essays.
8. Fiscal. 9. Fiscal postally used. 10. Grilled all over

PLATE 29.—PHILATELIC TERMS

1 and 2. Habilitado. 3. Holed. 4. Imprint on stamp. 5. Imprint on margin. 6. Interrupted perforation. 7. Interverted. 8. Ivory head. 9. Key plate. 10. Duty plate.

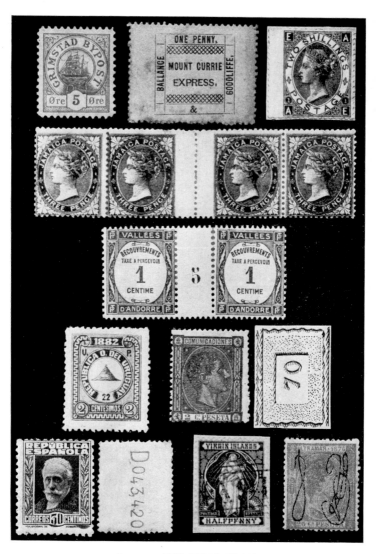

PLATE 30.—PHILATELIC TERMS

1 and 2. Locals. 3. Extended margin. 4. Pane margin divided by perforation causing extended margin. 5. Millésime. 6. Uruguay numbered on front. 7 and 8. Spain, framed number on back. and 9 and 10, rotation number on back. 11. Pantograph variety. 12. Paraph.

PLATE 31.—PHILATELIC TERMS

1. Pillars. 2 and 3. Postmasters' provisionals, Bermuda and St. Louis. 4, 5, and 6. Precancels. 7. Printers' waste. 8. Privilege stamp for Spanish Members of Parliament. 9. Retouch (on hills). 10. Serpentine roulette.

PLATE 32.—PHILATELIC TERMS

1 and 2. *Se tenant.* France two denominations, and Malta error "Pnney" with normal surcharge. 3. Set-off. 4. Overprint "Specimen." 5, 6, and 7. Split stamps, Canada and Mexico. 8 and 9. Stamp Currency front and back: Russia 10 and 11. *Tête-bêche,* France and Great Britain.

PART III
THE STUDY OF STAMPS

CHAPTER XV

POSTAGE STAMPS IN THE MAKING:
(A) DESIGN — ENGRAVING — PRINTING

WHILE IT IS POSSIBLE to collect stamps pleasurably and not unprofitably without going deeply into all the technicalities of their creation and manufacture, some general knowledge of the processes employed adds much to the appreciation of the variations in stamps. If the differences, and especially the aberrations, from the normal are worth collecting at all, it is useful and interesting to understand something of their causation.

An artist setting out to design a postage stamp works to a scale several times (commonly four or eight) the size of the stamp. His work must bear reduction to stamp size. A crowded design is liable to be a failure, but the authorities may have prescribed a number of devices and symbols, words and figures, to be incorporated. The artist should be advised beforehand by what printing process the stamps will be reproduced. A design to be engraved in recess on steel may contain more detail than if it is to be printed typographically. A still different treatment of the drawing will be required for an embossed, a lithographed, or a photogravure stamp.

The approved design, or a reduced photographic copy of it, has to be reproduced on to printing plates of metal or stone, or on metal cylinders, by diverse intermediate steps.

Line-engraving.—For steel-plate printing in recess the design is copied in reverse by a skilled engraver, who cuts the lines into the polished surface of a small flat block of steel. This is the die, in recess and reverse. It is submitted to a hardening process, and one or several copies of it are taken up on the broad edge of a (comparatively) soft steel roller. On the roller the lines of the design are in relief, and any inscription reads from left to right. This roller die after being hardened is rolled in as many times as required to a large steel plate capable of printing a full sheet. The designs as reproduced 100 or 200 or more on the plate are all replicas of the original die, and, like it, they are in recess and in reverse.

In printing the stamps from such plates, the ink is forced into the sunken recess lines and the level surface is wiped clean of ink. The paper is damp when it is brought in contact with the plate under pressure to make the impression.

This method of printing, which has been used for many stamps, including the historic first issues of Great Britain, is regarded by most philatelists as the most beautiful of stamp-printing processes.

In the course of a century little in the way of change has occurred in the practice of this process. Such changes as have been developing in recent years have been mechanical, and it is now possible to print such stamps rotary, in continuous reels and on dry instead of moist paper. For these the printing plates can be rolled in flat and then bent, allowing two to meet as one cylinder, or the roller die can be rolled direct into ready-made steel cylinders.

A general characteristic of stamps printed from such recess plates (*line-engraved* is the standard term for the method used by philatelists) is that the lines of the design appear to be standing up from the surface of the paper. Sometimes one finds on the back a slight corresponding indentation (without colour) of the design.

Typography.—For typographic printing the design may also be cut on steel, but in *relief*, an art which is much more difficult than engraving in recess, and has few successful practitioners. The best dies are made in this way, but woodcuts and photo-mechanical reliefs have been and are used.

The common method of multiplying the dies to compose the plates is by electrotyping, but stereotyping was much used in earlier days. In each case moulds are struck or cast from the die, and these moulds may be grouped or treated separately. In stereotyping, molten metal is poured over the moulds to form the printing surface. In electrotyping, the mould or group of moulds is placed in an electrolytic depositing bath, in which a thin film of copper is grown into the mould group. The shell of copper subsequently stripped from the moulds and backed with molten metal forms a plate on which the original die is reproduced the required number of times. The plate surface, being of pure copper, is too soft to stand the wear in printing large numbers of sheets of stamps, so it is generally surfaced with some harder and more durable metal—steel, nickel, or chromium—the coating being done by electro-deposition similar to that which produced the copper shell.

A plate of 100 or 240 or any given number of units, made in this way, and coated with one of the metals named, will stand long use in the printing press, and when the nickel or other surface begins to wear, that surface can be removed and a fresh one grown on to the original copper shell.

In typographic printing the relief lines of the design " bite " the paper, often indenting the lines, so that they can be seen to be slightly indented when examined from the back of the stamp. This is exactly the reverse of the slight embossing of the design seen on the back of a line-engraved stamp.

Embossing or die stamping is familiar to most people in its general principle, the relief being obtained by stamping the paper between an upper and a lower die. The matrix is cut on steel with the parts to be embossed in high relief cut out in deep recess. The counterpart die, or " force," may be of metal, or may be worked up from the matrix by stamping it on leather to force the paper into the recesses of the matrix.

Embossing has not been extensively used for adhesive postage stamps, although it is still used in Britain and other countries for stamped stationery. The early Great Britain embossed adhesive postage stamps (1847–54) were struck singly; a few foreign and colonial stamps have been embossed in the sheet, but the introduction of perforation has rendered the process impracticable. The high relief weakens the resistance of the paper, and interferes with the operation of the perforation.

Lithography, as the name implies, was originally a method of printing from stone (limestone), but excellent and more convenient substitutes for lithographic stones have been found in prepared thin plates of aluminium or zinc.

The stamp design may be drawn direct on the stone or transferred from prepared paper bearing the drawing, in lithographic ink, which is of a fat or greasy composition. The ink lines of the drawing adhere to the stone surface, and nothing less than mechanical force will remove them. A solution of gum with weak acid serves to set this image on the stone, closing up the pores where there is no ink and preventing the ink lines from spreading.

From this first copy on stone, transfers may be made on transfer paper. To obtain the transfers the protective gum is washed off the stone with water, leaving the ink lines undisturbed, as the grease repels water. A roller charged with greasy ink is passed over the wet stone; the ink only adheres to the lines of the design, the surface moisture repelling it everywhere else.

It is on the simple fact that grease and water will not mix that the whole principle of lithography rests.

From the drawing on stone a few or many transfers may be taken and retransferred on to larger stones, sufficient to provide a printing stone for a sheet of stamps. The paper transfers may be made up singly on a paper base, and transferred *en bloc* to the stone. It was a frequent practice with early stamp lithographers to make up a small group of transfers from the original to form an intermediate stone of five, ten, or twenty, from which further transfers were taken to compose the actual printing stones.

It will be remembered that each stage of transferring reverses the previous one, as to picture and inscription. The final, or printing stone, has the designs in reverse, so that when it is printed from, the design and inscription appear the right way on the sheet of stamps.

The process, being cheap and accessible in distant countries where facilities for other classes of printing were few, has been largely used. Many of the most interesting of the primitive issues of Europe, Asia, and South America were printed in this way from litho stones.

A lithographic impression is quite smooth and flat, and has neither the ink ridges of a line-engraving nor the bite and indenting of typographic printing.

Offset Lithography.—This process has been used not very successfully for stamps in the U.S.A., and with better results in Germany and some other countries. The impression obtained is as smooth as a lithograph. The units are built up by photographic means, and a positive metal plate is produced, which if printed direct on to paper would yield reversed stamps. The plate is inked, and the impression is taken off on a rubber-faced cylinder (the " blanket ") and it is offset from the rubber to the paper.

Photogravure.—With the huge output of the low-value

stamps of Great Britain printed by photogravure since 1934, this process has attained widespread recognition as a method of stamp printing which collectors should know something about. It has been in use for stamps of other countries, in varying forms and under a variety of trade or protected names, e.g. mechanical mezzotint (Bavaria, 1914 and 1920), heliogravure, collogravure, rotogravure.

The artist's design is photographed, stamp size, the glass negative is projected in a step and repeat machine the required number of times, to form a glass multi-positive, which is printed down on a sheet of carbon tissue on which has already been printed a fine screen of crossed lines.

The sheet of carbon tissue, bearing the number of images to form a sheet or more of stamps, is squeegeed damp on to a copper plate or cylinder, its paper base is removed, leaving the thin film of the images and screen upon the plate or cylinder. Washing removes the gelatine from the film everywhere except in those parts which have been acted upon by light, leaving these which are the images as a thin hard film on the copper. The plate or cylinder is then etched, an acid solution biting into the little squares, or cells, formed by the screen. The etching fluid acts lighter or deeper according to the varying tones of the image. The plate or cylinder has now the required number of stamp images, broken up into cells of varying depths. These cells hold the ink much in the same way as the recessed lines of steel-plate engraving; the paper is pressed into the images to take up the ink. Cylinders are coated with chromium to give them durability.

The inks used for making photogravure stamps have to be thin to be spread quickly to the cells of the images on the cylinders, and to allow a scraper to remove the surface ink in rapid rotary printing. The fluidity is obtained with xylol, a spirit of the benzine group, and the stamps are dry as soon as they are printed.

The character of the ink must be borne in mind by collectors who are accustomed to use the benzine cup for examining and cleaning stamps. The colour of photogravure stamps is liable to run in benzine.

The step and repeat machine is a precision projector apparatus, like a camera. When set it will project in rapid succession a stamp image on a sensitised plate as many times as required, with uniform spacing and alignment. It " steps " out a horizontal row, then moves back and " repeats " for each subsequent row.

It is now extensively used for most of the stamp-printing processes where the printing plates can be produced by photography and etching.

CHAPTER XVI

POSTAGE STAMPS IN THE MAKING: (B) PAPER—WATERMARK—GUM— PERFORATION—SHEETS—BOOKLETS— COILS

PAPER IS AN IMPORTANT factor in the study of stamps, both as to the character of the paper itself and the watermark, if any, that it shows. Many kinds of paper altogether unsuitable for stamps have been used in emergencies, from the coarse blue sugar paper in which Demerara sugar is wrapped to the thinnest of cigarette papers. Many specially devised " safety " or patent papers have been used, some of them only experimentally, and most of those we need to know about are listed in the concluding section of this book.

Here we have to describe briefly how paper is made, how it gets its texture, and its watermark.

Plant life is the basis of all pulping material for making paper. The best papers are made from cotton and linen rags, cheaper grades from esparto grass, spruce trees, straw, and other resources of the vegetable kingdom. These materials are all fibrous; they are cleared of impurities, boiled and " digested," bleached and beaten up to separate every fibre. In the beating operation dyes may be intro-duced for coloured papers.

The soft fibrous mass obtained is the dry pulp, which when water is added forms a thick semi-liquid pulp. For hand-made paper, a mahogany frame, across which is stretched a fine wire cloth, held in by a deckle, is dipped into the pulp vat, shaken to let the superfluous water pass through the sieve-like wire, and there is the sheet of moist paper; turned out on to a damp felt, it is pressed and dried.

The deckle, which temporarily converted the framed wire cloth into a kind of tray, determines the size of the sheet of paper. The wire cloth itself determines the texture of the paper : if the wire is woven like cloth, the paper will be " wove." If, however, the wire is formed of parallel lines close together, and only crossed for support at wide intervals, the sheet of paper takes this texture, and is known as " laid."

The wire cloth that gives the sheet of hand-made paper its texture also gives it the watermark device, formed by " bits " of wire fashioned to shape, and sewn on the wire cloth.

It is in texture and the watermark that we are chiefly interested.

Machine-made paper is formed by flowing the wet pulp on to a moving band of wire cloth. The flow is limited in the lateral direction by deckle straps moving at the same rate ; these deckles determine the width of the web of paper. The moving band, with its coating of wet pulp, is kept vibrating sideways to shake out superfluous moisture.

As the pulp approaches the other end of the moving wire cloth it is still soft and moist, and in this state it passes under the dandy roll, which gives the paper its texture and its watermark.

The dandy roll is a cylinder of wire cloth, and if this cloth be wove, the paper will be " wove "; if it is laid, the paper will be " laid." On this cylinder also the wire " bits " fashioned for watermark devices are sewn.

The dandy roll moving over the travelling film of partly formed paper, carefully regulated to give just the right amount of pressure, thus impresses the texture and the watermark. The web of paper after passing under the dandy is led off on a band of felt to pressing rollers and drying cylinders.

The philatelist should remember the fibrous character of the paper. The process of manufacture has tended to make the fibres lie parallel in the direction of the web. If you take a sheet of dry paper and wet it, you will find that it has expanded, but the expansion is not proportionate in each direction. What happens is that the fibres, being like fine tubes, fill with moisture; they do not lengthen, they swell. Thus the paper expands more in the " cross " direction than in the direction of the web. The fibres shrink again when dry, but both expansion and shrinkage being variable, paper which has been damped for line-engraved printing, and again damped by gumming, will show slight variations in the size of the stamp impressions, leading collectors at times to believe the differences are due to the use of different dies. This uneven shrinkage of paper makes it difficult for the perforating to be kept centred in the perforation gutters.

We have seen how the watermark is introduced into the paper. Now we may examine some of the kinds of watermarks we find in stamps. Not all stamps are printed on watermarked paper, and some are on paper which only has a paper-maker's watermark in the sheet.

Nearly all British stamps from 1840 to 1912 had one watermark to each stamp. Early in the reign of King George V a departure was made in introducing the royal cypher as a watermark. This passed through several stages:

1   2

3

1. Simple. The device with script letters is repeated in even columns.

2. Multiple. Same device, but spread in alternate columns.

3. Multiple Roman. The stamps of King Edward VIII are watermarked on the multiple Roman plan E 8 R, and those of King George VI : G VI R. The Queen Elizabeth II watermark was E 2 R. The current watermark is multiple crowns, but the new " Queen " definitives introduced in 1967 are without watermark.

The multiple watermark has superseded the single device per stamp kind of watermark. On the multiple plan, which the paper-makers call the " all-over " watermark, no stamp can very well miss getting parts of two or more of the devices.

The multiple watermark came into use for stamps supplied to the order of the Crown Agents for the Colonies before it was adopted for Great Britain. The following is the sequence of the chief watermarks in the Crown Colonies group. CC stands for Crown Colonies ; CA for Crown Agents.

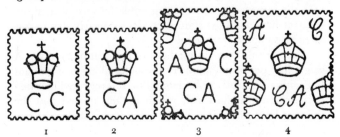

1   2   3   4

1. Crown CC, *circa* 1863–82.
2. Crown CA (single), 1882–1904.
3. Multiple CA 1904–*circa* 1926.
4. Multiple Script CA, 1921–*circa* 1965.
5. Multiple Capital CA and St. Edward's Crown, 1957–.

The watermarks to be found in the stamps of the Dominions and of foreign countries are of many designs, " single " or " multiple," with an increasing trend to the multiple or " all-over " watermark. Network and inter-laced patterns all over the paper have been much used of late. All these things will reveal themselves to you if you look beyond the designs on your stamps.

In early times the gum used for stamps was applied by hand with brushes on the sheets after printing, but before perforating. Later on machine gumming became the prac-tice, the coating of gum being applied to one side of the paper much in the same way as the surface of the paper might be given a surface colour, or a chalk coating.

For many years the typographed stamps of Great Britain were printed on paper already gummed. It was found that typographic plates gave better impressions on gummed paper, but there were other advantages, in speeding up manufacture and in securing good register in the perfor-ating machines.

For line-engraved stamps, until modern times, the print-ing had to be done first because the paper had to be damp to take the impression. Now it is possible by several methods to print line-engraved stamps on dry or nearly dry paper, already gummed in the reel.

There are three main methods of perforating stamps. A single-line perforator punches the holes along one straight line, either vertically or horizontally. It is repeated between each row down the sheet, which is then turned and the crossing lines perforated in the same way. Collectors can generally distinguish stamps perforated this way, as there is a clash at each point of juncture where the perforations cross.

Diagram showing the punctures made at one blow of a " comb " machine; the centre narrow division marks the dividing space between two panes of British colonial stamps.

The comb principle of perforating, the best method devised as yet, perforates along the full length or width of the sheet, its spurs also perforating the sides of the stamps. The next blow of the perforator completes the first row of stamps, and the spurs do the sides of the next row. The process is repeated down the sheet. It is not quite so slow as it seems, for six or seven sheets go through the comb at one time.

With the comb properly set, each blow of the perforator completes the previous one, and there is no cross or clash. To complete the last row or column the spurs run out into the margin.

The third method is the harrow perforation, where the perforation punches are set to perforate a full sheet at one operation. This has not been extensively used, as it presents considerable mechanical difficulties, and is not regarded as economic in the matter of repair. Switzerland, the one country that used this method over a long period, turned to the comb principle about 1914. A sheet of stamps perforated in the harrow style rarely has any perforations extending into any of the sheet margin.

Rotary perforating is akin to the single line, for although there will be a number of wheels bearing punches, working into other wheels bored with holes, they work in one direction at a time, and have to be cross-perforated by another set of wheels. The crossing is marked by the irregular-shaped holes where the perforations meet.

The comb perforators have long been adapted for perforating in the web, and modern developments have been the multiple comb, perforating three, four, or five rows at a time, and leaving spurred perforations for the next descent of the comb.

Rouletting, an early substitute for perforating, was done by hand wheels which pricked or cut the paper. The like effect and purpose can also be achieved by raised printers' rules which make similar pricks or cuts.

The use of the perforation gauge for measuring stamp perforations and roulettes is described in Chapter II.

.   .   .   .   .

Postage stamps were first printed and issued to the post offices in sheets of 240, a convenient figure for the sterling currency. A sheet of 240 1d. stamps represented £1, and each of the twenty rows represented 1s. Countries using decimal currencies find 100 or multiples of 100 more convenient. There have been " sheets " composed of single stamps, and others in a range of sizes, from four units to 960, but the large sheets are usually printers' sheets, which are cut up into post office or issue sheets.

The issue sheets are often rendered capable of easy division, by what we term panes. For many years our English sheets of 240 were arranged in two panes of 120 each, one pane above the other, with a pillared margin cancelling the watermarked paper between the panes. Many of the British colonial stamps are printed in sheets of 240, divided into four panes of sixty. The printing plates were so made that they could be used to print the low values in sheets of 240 for very large editions, or 120 for smaller editions, while the high values, of which only small quantities are required, can be worked in sheets of sixty.

Some curiously irregular sizes or arrangements of sheets are met with, generally, but not always, due to an economising of either printing surface or paper. Lithographers having laid down a rectangular grouping of transfers on their stone, finding they have rather more space than is required, have filled up with a few more transfers, sometimes set sideways to fit them in. Colombia affords several examples. The Roumanian stamps of 1870–72 were lithographed in sheets of 100, formed of two rows of fifteen and five rows of fourteen. Other lithographed Roumanian stamps were in similarly irregular sheets.

In the case of the early Austrian typographed stamps printed in sheets of sixty, the stamps are in eight rows of eight, but the bottom row is reduced to four stamps, the remaining four spaces being printed with St. Andrew's crosses in colour. In a later issue (1858) the cross is uncoloured on a solid ground. These " cross " stamps have sometimes puzzled beginners, especially in the perforated stamps.

Stamps are still printed and issued in sheets, but two other methods of issue have been developed in the twentieth century. These are the handy booklets of stamps, and the issue in coil form for use in automatic vending and affixing machines.

The first booklets of stamps for general use were issued in the United States on April 16th, 1900, and achieved popular favour from the first. Great Britain issued booklets on March 16th, 1904, and the system has been very widely adopted for low-value stamps in most countries and colonies. The British issue of 1904 was in booklets of twenty-four 1d. stamps, which sold for 2s. 0½d., the odd halfpenny being a charge to cover the extra cost of manufacture. In 1906 the contents of the booklets provided twelve 1d. and twenty-three $\frac{1}{2}d$. stamps; where the twenty-fourth $\frac{1}{2}d$. stamp might have been was a space cancelled with a St. Andrew's cross. It has been nicknamed the " kiss stamp." The price was then 2s. per booklet, the missing $\frac{1}{2}d$. stamp representing the cost.

There were other adjustments, but not until the introduction of the King George V booklets in 1911, when the $\frac{1}{2}d$. charge for manufacture was abandoned, did the British booklets achieve great popularity (see page 66).

Improvements in mechanical appliances for the automatic vending of stamps, and apparatus for the rapid affixing of stamps on large mailings, led to the issue of stamps in coils or rolls suitable for delivery by these machines. They came into use in America in 1908 and in Britain in 1912. The early coils were made by pasting sheets end to end, but modern rotary printing makes that unnecessary. The wide web of printed stamps is slit up into single ribbons of the required lengths and coiled up on spools.

British stamps with black graphite lines on the back were introduced in 1957 in connection with the experimental use of automatic letter-facing machines (used for sorting electronically) at Southampton. These stamps were followed by the issue of others in 1959 with almost-invisible phosphor bands on the face of the stamps which, definitive and commemorative, are in current use in place of the normal stamps in the Southampton, London S.E., Liverpool and Glasgow areas etc., where letter-facing machines have been installed. Their use will gradually be extended to the whole of the United Kingdom. All British stamps, ordinary and commemorative, now bear phosphor bands.

CHAPTER XVII

REMAINDERS—REPRINTS—
OFFICIAL IMITATIONS

IT IS ALMOST UNAVOIDABLE that a postal administration in
launching a new issue of stamps will be left with some
residue of the stamps that are being superseded. Philatelists can have no quarrel with the bona fide remainder,
which is not just equal to but is the original article. The
sale of a remainder stock may affect temporarily the
value of the stamps on the market: it is not the primary
concern of a postal administration to consider the stamp
market.

The sale of remainder stocks in early days has permitted
a moderate proportion of fine old stamps to remain accessible to the modern stamp collector. That is something to be
thankful for when so many of the old stamps have soared
in price.

Properly, a remainder is the surplus stock of completed
stamps in the post offices, in the Government treasuries,
and at the printers. Even the unfinished stamps at the
printers, if duly completed for inclusion in the remainder
stock, are admissible.

From the official point of view, a Government selling a
remainder stock of an issue which has been demonetised or
invalidated for use is quite entitled to sell it for what can be
got for it. That implies in most cases less than the original
face value, the stamps having been deprived of further value
in use.

There are excellent alternative methods for a Government
to dispose of remainders. In Great Britain the practice is
to allow the stock of one issue to become exhausted in

ordinary use, concurrently with the gradual distribution of the new stock. A similar process of exhaustion is pursued in other great countries, but in many cases supersession of one issue has not involved demonetisation.

Another alternative way of disposing of surplus stock is to destroy it. In many cases this is probably the best solution, although at times it plays into the hands of speculators, and at others deprives us of the opportunity of getting specimens for our own collections.

We may agree that unused remainders, being originals, are welcome additions to our collections, and we do not quarrel with the opportunity of getting them more cheaply than if there had been no remainders.

A different case arises when a Government selling a remainder stock lends itself to giving that stock the *suggestio falsi* of having been used in the post. There was no misrepresentation when Mauritius sold the remainders of the 1860–73 issue overprinted with the word " Cancelled." Switzerland overprinted remainders of 1881 " ausser kurs " (out of use). On the other hand, when a stock of over 2,000,000 of British South Africa Company's issues for Rhodesia was " postmarked " in London in 1924 with date marks from 1897 to 1912, it was not in my opinion a legitimate proceeding. Similarly, the remainder of the two " Victoria Land " overprinted on New Zealand stamps issued to the British Antarctic Expedition of 1911–13 were sold in London in 1913, and were offered mint, or they would be obligingly postmarked for you with the historic date January 18th, 1913, 1.30 p.m., when the *Terra Nova* arrived at the post office at Cape Evans, Victoria Land, on her last relief voyage.

To sum up, remainders are best taken unused, next cancelled by overprint or dumb cancellation, while those with fictitiously dated postmarks are best left out.

Reprints are posthumous printings of stamps, made after the issue of those stamps has ceased. That is a generalisation rather than a definition, for there is much more for the collector to understand about them.

A true reprint must derive from the same original printing surface, die, plate, or stone as the original stamps. In a large number of cases of reprinting the original plates or stones have not been available, and new ones have been made from the original die. This is one distinct remove from a true reprint, but so long as they have their source in the original die they are still classed as reprints, although they are of less interest in philatelic study.

In some instances Governments have ordered reprints of obsolete stamps for exhibition or presentation purposes or to meet a demand from collectors, after all the original printing material, including the dies, have been destroyed. Where a new die has been engraved, or an old one altered, to make new plates or stones, the result is an " Official Imitation," a politer term than Government counterfeit. Even Governments cannot reproduce their own obsolete stamps by re-engraving them with such fidelity that they cannot be distinguished from the originals. Such stamps, although manufactured and sold as " reprints," are not reprints at all, and stand in a class by themselves. A reprint must retain a link with the original, and not be a copy.

There are two main classes of true reprints, the first made under authority by the Government, and the second made by private persons or firms which have purchased or otherwise acquired some or all of the requisite printing material. Those made under authority are of superior interest; those made by private concerns vary greatly in interest, and some have been printed with such prodigality as to be not much better than litter.

What should be the collector's attitude to bona fide

reprints? In the space-filling days of the general collector using the old-fashioned printed album there were many who considered that a true reprint was better than an empty space. There is no reason why they should not continue to do so, provided they do not deceive themselves or others.

Among specialists in the stamps of any country of whose stamps reprints exist, a knowledge of them is necessary. Where the reprints are from original *plates* (they rarely come from original *stones*), they show the same lay-out and general characteristics of those plates and are valuable for study. Where a stamp or series has been reprinted on several occasions, the specialist studies the characteristics of each separate printing.

The one drawback for the young collector in the matter of reprints is that there are people who will try to palm reprints off on them as originals. Fortunately the catalogues generally give notes of what reprints exist, and the most ready means of distinguishing them. It is impossible to give a detailed list of reprints here; there are far too many. They rarely match the originals in every detail. Starting with the actual original plate, it may have got scratched or corroded in storage. Then the paper is rarely to be matched exactly—it may be whiter or more toned than that used for the originals. Colours present other difficulties in reprinting after the original formula has been lost, and it is in their colour differences that reprints proclaim themselves most readily. Even the gum—for reprints are usually encountered " mint "—is such a minor detail that the maker of reprints has given little thought to the matching of it. Then, finally, there is the perforation (if any), which is often of a different gauge.

CHAPTER XVIII

FORGERIES AND FRAUDS—
HOW EXPERTS WORK

FORGERIES OF POSTAGE STAMPS are of two main groups:

1. Forgeries intended for use in the post, to the detriment of Government revenue.

2. Forgeries made to deceive collectors.

The former class includes counterfeits of historical and technical interest. To the specialist there is an incentive to procure and study forgeries which have actually passed in the post; on many occasions it has been due to the penetrating observation of philatelists that the circulation of fraudulent stamps has been discovered.

So there is an academic interest for the collector for what are generally and simply styled *faux pour servir*.

Spain and a few of the old Italian States probably suffered most from forgeries. Some of the Latin-American countries also. Great Britain has rarely suffered from the attentions of the stamp forger; comparative immunity has been due to the strict system of distribution and control over the sale of stamps. All reasonable care has been taken in manufacture to present the utmost difficulty in close imitation, but imitations need not be very close to pass among the millions of letters handled every day. Hence the importance of the distribution and control of sale to post offices and licensed vendors of stamps. The forger of a 1d. stamp can only make it profitable by producing large quantities, and under the British system it is next to impossible to market such quantities without early discovery.

The modern collector has nothing to fear from forgeries that have been used in the post. Few of them ever come on the stamp market, and in nearly all cases they are much rarer than the genuine stamps, although only of interest to the specialist.

·   ·   ·   ·   ·

Forgeries have been made in great variety to deceive collectors; they began to make their appearance almost as soon as stamp collecting first attracted public interest in the early 'sixties. Nearly coincidental with the first printed catalogues of stamps for collectors, there were several little companion works listing the forgeries that were known.

In later times facsimiles have been manufactured and marked as such, bearing a tiny inscription or overprint, e.g. facsimile, false, falsch, faux; they are not to be regarded as more honest than the unmarked kind, for the mark may be skilfully removed, or more simply covered by a forged postmark, and the only commercial use for such facsimiles has been to pass them on as genuine. The overprint has served as a screen for the maker. When challenged with making forgeries, he can claim they were facsimiles and marked as such, and it is difficult to prove that he also sold quantities, at a higher rate, without the tell-tale marks.

Today the market conditions do not lend themselves to so general a circulation of fakes. The early dealers, like the early collectors, had little to guide them; they were both very much in the dark. Now the leading stamp firms pride themselves on a wide and expert knowledge, and take every care to guard their reputations and ensure that the stamps they sell are what they represent them to be. They guarantee the stamps they sell, and the modern stamp collector dealing with reputable stamp firms need not fear the bogy of " fudges."

Be wary of what appear to be very old collections in antiquated albums, the stamps glued down to the pages.

There is a glamour attaching to the " Lallier " album, the first album specially published for stamp collectors, for many a time rarities have been discovered in them. Inexperienced collectors are easily deceived by the age of the album; they presume it is so old that the stamps must be genuine, whereas the cheap forgeries described above were more commonly accessible than they are today. Nowadays, although the discovery of a collection in an oblong Lallier album always piques our interest, one must guard against the contents being faked up with forgeries of clever modern manufacture, and with repaired stamps.

. . . . .

More troublesome than outright forgeries are forged surcharges on genuine stamps, and fakes made in attempting to turn common stamps into supposedly rare varieties. The latter include some very cunning impostures. An early trick was to take an ordinary 1d. black stamp of 1840, and after erasing the little star ornaments in the top angles printing in their place the letters V and R, in imitation of the scarce " VR " stamp prepared in 1840 for official use, but never brought into use (compare Stamps 1 and 3 on Plate 1). The popular demand for errors led to fakers providing " inverted centres " by taking the normal stamp, cutting out the centre, and more or less skilfully putting it back in the inverted position.

More subtle alterations now come before the experts for opinion. The use of standard key-plate designs for stamps of many colonies and long ranges of denominations has been cleverly turned to account. An audacious example discovered a few years ago was the £25 King Edward VII stamp of Northern Nigeria, 1904, printed in green and carmine. The key-plate was printed in green; the duty-plate bearing the name of the colony and the denomination is in carmine. The fake was made by taking a cheap stamp —the 1 cent green Straits Settlements of the King Edward series. From this the faker cleared the top and bottom tablets of the duty-plate impression and inserted " Northern Nigeria " for " Straits Settlements " at the top and the " £25 " for " 1c. " at the bottom. He made two mistakes. The 1 cent green Straits Settlements stamp has the old single CA watermark; the £25 Northern Nigeria should have the multiple CA watermark. The other mistake was a glaring one; a duty-plate of the wrong type was used.

· The forger can do little in the matter of faking water-marks; it is done, but not very successfully. In a very few cases he has secured a sheet or two of original watermarked paper, but more commonly he depends upon being able to discharge the colour from a cheap stamp having the appropriate watermark. A modern forgery of the £10 British Central Africa (now Nyasaland Protectorate) of 1897 has the Crown CC watermark, but to get this the faker has taken a common fiscal stamp, which has the wrong perforation compound 15 by 14, instead of the correct perf. 14.

A not uncommon kind of fraud is the cleaning of stamps which have been used, for sale as unused. Postmarks are not easily removed, but pen-cancellations on early line-engraved stamps which have been used for fiscal purposes are often cleaned and offered either as unused, or provided with false postmarks. A stamp that has been cleaned will often betray itself to the naked eye, for however easy it is to remove the colour from a penmark, the nib leaves its mark in scratches, and the faking of fresh gum on the back can, if necessary, be subjected to certain simple tests.

For nearly all fakes of conversion of stamps from common to rare varieties such as I have described in this chapter, and for " cleaned " stamps, as well as damaged stamps which have been skilfully repaired, the expert has valuable help from photography, and still more from the quartz lamp, generating ultra-violet rays. Almost any kind of tampering with the colour, paper pen-scratches, postmark, or the joins and mucilage used in repairing damaged stamps, reveal themselves under fluorescence tests with these lamps, which are now at the service of the expert committees and the leading stamp dealers. Many private collectors have installed them, but such accessories would be unnecessary luxuries for the average collector, who is not seriously menaced by the forgery and fakery of stamps so long as he uses ordinary common sense in buying, and deals in the main with firms of standing.

CHAPTER XIX

THE STAMP COLLECTOR'S VOCABULARY

ADHESIVE.—A stamp which has to be affixed to a letter or postal packet by means of gum or other mucilage, as distinct from a stamp actually printed on the envelope, post card, or wrapper.

AERO-PHILATELY.—The study and collection of air stamps, as a branch of philately.

AIR STAMP.—A stamp issued expressly for use on mail transported by air.

ALBINO.—A term applied in its general dictionary sense to an impression without colour from an uninked stamp die or plate or from printers' type.

ANILINE.—A colourless liquid chemical base used in the production of brilliant colours. Stamps printed in aniline inks generally show some saturation of the paper, which may show through to the back.

ARROW, ARROW-BLOCK.—Arrows, and similar marks, printed

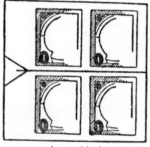

Arrow-block

in the margins of sheets as register marks for printer and perforator, or as guides in dividing up sheets. An arrow-block consists of four or more stamps, with margin showing the arrow.

AUTOMATIC PERFORATION.—Stamps are supplied in rolls or coils for use in different types of automatic vending or affixing machines. In early experimental types of these machines the stamps were supplied imperforate, or perforated in one direction only, the machine effecting a perforation at its delivery end. Compare INTERRUPTED PERFORATION.

BACK-STAMPED.—The dated postmark of arrival at post office of destination, when present, is usually found on the back of a cover.

BALLON MONTÉ.—A balloon with pilot. BALLON NON MONTÉ.—
A free balloon. During the siege of Paris, 1870-71, a higher rate of
postage was charged for mail sent *par ballon monté*, but the service
by free balloons was a failure. See PAPILLONS.

BARRED.—Cancelled with bars to render stamps (generally
remainders) invalid for postal use (Plate 27, Stamp 1).

BATONNÉ PAPER.—Watermarked with lines not close together,
but as if ruled for guidance in writing.

BISECT, BISECTED PROVISIONAL.—A stamp cut in half (vertically,
horizontally, or diagonally) for use at half the face value of the
whole. The bisection by the public may be sanctioned by
authority, during a shortage of stamps of the lower denomination.
In some cases the bisecting is done, and accompanied by a surcharge, by the issuing authority (Plate 27, Stamps 2 and 3).
See also SPLIT STAMPS.

BLEUTÉ PAPER.—Paper which has acquired a bluish tinge in
its manufacture, or subsequently through chemical reaction set
up by prussiate of potash in the printing ink. See IVORY HEAD.

BLOCK.—An unsevered group of stamps, not fewer than four,
thus ⊞. Compare STRIP.

BLOCK.—A unit for typographic printing, e.g. wood-block, line-,
or half-tone block, stereo, zinco, or electro.

BLUED PAPER.—See BLEUTÉ.

BOGUS.—A label which, while purporting to be a postage
stamp, never had any genuine existence as such. A genuine
stamp may have a *bogus surcharge*, i.e. a surcharge added without
sanction of authority.

BOOKLETS, BOOKLET LEAF, BOOKLET SHEET.—Stamps issued in
handy booklet form are printed in large sheets laid out on a
different plan from the regular sheets, for convenience in cutting
up and binding into booklets. A BOOKLET SHEET is the full sheet
that has not been cut up. A BOOKLET LEAF is one of the small
leaves (or blocks) of stamps of which a booklet is composed.

BOTH SIDES, stamps printed on.—Stamps printed on both sides
(not set-offs) are of interest to collectors. They are distinguished
from set-offs in having both impressions reading correctly from
left to right, while a set-off is reversed. These " both sides "
stamps are occasionally errors, but more often are due to economy

in the use of paper ; the printer finding his sheet inadequately printed (insufficiently inked, etc.) turns the sheet and prints a better impression on the other side. Some curious examples are described in Chapter VII.

BUREAU PRINT (U.S.).—Stamps precancelled at the Bureau of Engraving and Printing before delivery to the Post Office are so distinguished from stamps precancelled locally by postmasters.

BURELAGE, BURELÉ.—A reticulated or network pattern. Such patterns often form part of a stamp design, but the terms are

Burelage

Figs. 1 and 2.—Denmark and Danish West Indies.　　Fig. 3.—Queensland, on back.

chiefly applied in philately to such patterns printed as protective underprints before the stamps are printed, e.g. as in Figs. 1 and 2, Denmark and Danish West Indies; and as Fig. 3 on the back of Queensland stamps.

CACHET.—A mark impressed by hand-stamp (and rarely printed) on envelope or card to denote the special circumstances in which it has been posted, e.g. on an important expedition, on a particular air flight, at an exposition, or to denote first day of use of a stamp, or a particular anniversary or event. The cachet may be official, i.e. applied by the Post Office, or private if applied independently of Post Office authority.

Small marks stamped by experts, dealers, and collectors on the backs of stamps as marks of guarantee, authenticity, or identification, generally in the form of initials, are also CACHETS.

CANCELLATION.—Any mark applied to a stamp to prevent its use, or re-use, in the post, e.g. a postmark, pen cancellation, an overprint or manuscript addition denoting invalidation, e.g. Cancelled, Specimen, Sample, Inutilizado, or mute cancellations (see BARRED) or punched with holes (see HOLED). A mute can-

piece " (of cover, wrapper, etc.). An envelope or wrapper w[hich] has been carried by air mail is a " flown cover." See also [?] STAMP COVERS.

C.P., COPPER-PLATE.—The initials commonly met with official announcements of stamps denoting they are printed the copper-plate method, although not necessarily from plate copper. See LINE-ENGRAVING.

CUBIERTAS.—Large labels affixed to insured letters in Colon and several Colombian States. Of two kinds: 1, value declared, and 2, value declared. About 100 varieties used t[o] catalogued, but they are not strictly postage stamps (Plate Stamp 1).

CURRENT NUMBER.—A number printed in the margin[s] British and colonial and some foreign sheets of stamps sho[w] the sequence of plates made at the printers' works, independ[ent] of duty (face value), purpose (postal, telegraph, or fiscal), o[r] the country or colony for which the plate was provided. It is to be confused with either " control " or the " plate numb[er] (Plate 28, Stamp 12).

CUT-OUTS.—Impressed stamps cut out from envelopes, [?] cards, wrappers, or other printed postal stationery, for use ordinary stamps, or for collecting purposes.

CUT-SQUARE.—Cut-outs are usually cut square, or rath[er] rectangular, not close round the design. Where adhesive stam[ps] are of peculiar external form, e.g. round, oval, or octagonal, th[ey] are at their best when cut square (Plate 28).

CUT TO SHAPE.—A stamp of unusual form, e.g. round, ov[al] octagonal, etc., trimmed close to the conformation of the impr[es]sion. Stamps which have been mutilated in this way are relativ[ely] valueless compared with those which have been cut squa[re] (Plate 28).

CYLINDER NUMBER.—British stamp sheets printed by rota[ry] photogravure from cylindrical plates bear small figures in t[he] [l]ower left margin, below the control, denoting the number of t[he] [c]ylinder (Plate 27, Stamp 13).

DEMONETISED.—Obsolete stamps which have been specifical[ly] [d]eprived of validity in the post and of redemption value. [?] [G]reat Britain stamps of the reigns of Queen Victoria and Ki[ng] [E]dward VII have been demonetised.

cellation is a postmark void of inscription, letters, or figures, in U.S. a " killer."

CANCELLED BY COMPLAISANCE.—Stamps postmarked to oblige collectors.

CANCELLED TO ORDER.—Stamps postmarked in quantities for sale to the stamp trade, without giving any postal service in return.

CANTONAL STAMPS.—Postage stamps issued by cantonal administrations prior to the general adoption of the system by the Swiss Confederation (Plate 1).

CARNET.—French for " booklet " (q.v.) CARNETISME.—The collection and study of stamp booklets.

CARRIERS' STAMPS.—Early stamps of the United States (1842–59) denoting the letter-carriers' charges for the delivery of mail to or from a post office in the locality in which the carriers' stamps were issued. At that period, in many parts of the country there was no house-to-house delivery or collection of mail. The carriers provided a link between the post-office service and the addressee, where the latter could not conveniently collect his own mail at the post office, or deliver his outward mail there. The " Franklin " and " Eagle " stamps were Government issues, some others were provided by the local postmasters, and still others by the letter-carriers on their own responsibility (Plate 27, Stamp 5).

CATALOGUE.—The principal standard catalogues of postage stamps serve collectors as comparative guides to the values of stamps. Originally they were dealers' price lists; they are still that, inasmuch as they represent the dealer's selling prices for stamps in stock. They are now more than that, and give approximate prices, based on transactions and the available information, even in the case of the majority of stamps which are not in stock. The expression " catalogue value " is commonly used when " catalogue price " is meant, and can only be taken as a rough guide to true value, in which condition and other factors are taken into account.

CEMENT.—Instructions engraved in the margins of sheets of early stamps of Great Britain advised: " In wetting the Back be careful not to remove the Cement," i.e. the gum.

CENTRED.—A stamp is *well centred* when the impression lies evenly between the perforated edges on all four sides. The antonym is " off centre " (Plate 27, Stamps 6 and 7).

CHALK LINES.—An underprint of intersecting lines of chalky character served a dual purpose in Russia (1909) of preventing the cleaning of used stamps, and making it difficult to counterfeit the stamps by photography. See also QUADRILLÉ, and VARNISH LINES.

Chalk lines.

CHALKY, OR CHALK-SURFACED PAPER.—Indicated in many catalogues by the initial " C." This is a paper which has been coated on the printing side with a solution of chalk and gum or size; it produces a more brilliant but more fugitive colour impression. Compare FUGITIVE.

CHANGELING.—A stamp whose colour or shade of colour, or paper, has been changed by chemical or other reaction. The change may be accidental—some inks change colour in water—or at times fraudulent.

CHECK LETTERS.—Letters in the corners of early British stamps arranged in double alphabetical sequence throughout each sheet, so that no two stamps on a sheet bore an identical combination. The letters were at first in the two lower corners, but later the upper corners were provided with letters which are the same as in the lower corners, but in reverse order. See Chapter IX.

CIGARETTE PAPER.—Thin semi-transparent paper, without gum, e.g. Latvia, 1919.

CLEANED STAMP.—One which has had its first cancellation (generally a pen or rubber-stamp cancellation) removed by chemical or other agency. Stamps, especially of high denominations used chiefly for fiscal purposes, are often " cleaned " and provided with forged postmarks. Collectors must beware of these, as also of early rare engraved stamps which have been " cleaned " and offered as unused.

CLICHÉ.—One of the separate units (stereo or electro) making up a plate for printing stamps.

COILS, COIL FORM.—The U.S. Post Office issues stamps in coil form, or coils; the British Post Office does likewise, but calls them " rolls of stamps." They are printed on wide reels, which are then mechanically slit into single-width ribbons, and are coiled up on separate spools to the required length, and sealed. Stamps issued in coil form may often present differences from the like stamps issued in sheet or booklet form.

COLOUR TRIALS.—Proofs in colour made by stamp printers for experimental purposes, and to enable officials to make a suitable selection of colours.

COLUMN.—The vertical lines of stamps in a sheet are described as *columns*, the horizontal lines as *rows*.

COMBINATION COVER.—One that has been prepaid with stamps of two or more countries, chiefly found among early letters when the stamps of one country were not valid beyond its own borders.

COMB MACHINE PERFORATION.—The work of a machine which at each blow perforates three sides of each stamp in one row; a second blow, after the paper has been moved up, completes th perforating of the first row, and so on to the bottom of the shee See Chapter XVI.

COMMEMORATIVE.—A stamp issued in commemoration of som event or anniversary.

COMPOUND PERFORATION.—When the gauge of the perforati on a stamp is not the same all round, it is a compound perforat Usually a compound perforation consists of only two differe of gauge, the top and bottom being in one gauge, and the in another. In describing such a perforation in the catalogu horizontal perforation (i.e. at top and bottom) is mentione and the sides next—thus " compound perforation 15 by 1 " 15 × 14."

CONTROL.—A record letter, or letter with number, prir the margin of the sheet, as in bottom or left side margin o stamp sheets from $\frac{1}{2}d.$ to 1s. The large figures accompan control letter indicate year of printing, thus: 38=1938 (F

Sheets of some foreign stamps bear divers marginal m in checking production, or other control.

CORNER BLOCK.—A block of stamps with margins corner of a sheet, of interest chiefly when the stamps quarter are abnormal, or when the margin shows a co number, or date.

CORNER LETTERS.—See CHECK LETTERS.

COVER.—The envelope or wrapper. A stamp reta whole envelope is " on original cover," or " on enti a portion of the cover remains, the stamp is descr

DENOMINATION.—The face value, as expressed in words or figures on a stamp.

DENTELÉ.—French for perforated. NON-DENTELÉ.—Imperforate. DENTELURE.—The perforation. The gauge of a perforation is given as " Dent(elure) 12." See PERFORATION.

DEOXIDISE.—See DESULPHURATE.

DEPARTMENTAL STAMPS.—Stamps designed, or appropriated by overprinting, for use of Government departments. The word " Department " or contraction " Dept." figures on the several series of stamps (except the " Executive ") supplied to the U.S. Departments from 1873—State, Treasury, War, Navy, etc.—so Americans and collectors of U.S. stamps call them Departmentals. See also OFFICIAL STAMPS.

DESULPHURATE.—Some printing inks derived from metallic bases are liable to become impregnated with sulphur. Stamps printed in such inks are often affected, becoming unevenly deepened in shade, or turning brownish black, or black. To desulphurate them, restoring them to their original colour, they are treated with peroxide of hydrogen in solution.

DICKINSON PAPER.—Named after its inventor, this paper, used for the Mulready and other envelopes, and in rare cases for adhesive stamps, has continuous silk threads embedded in it. A device intended as an obstacle to counterfeiters.

DIE.—The original plate or block bearing the design engraved in correct dimension is the *original* or *master die*. It is used sparingly, to provide duplicates sufficient to become (after additions to the engraving) master dies for each of the several denominations in a series. These may be transferred by means of *roller dies* to a steel plate, or to provide *working dies* to make moulds for electrotyping. See Chapter XV.

The terms Die I, Die II, etc., are used to distinguish actual stamps deriving from dies, or replicas of dies, which have been subjected to small alterations.

DIE PROOF.—A carefully printed impression from a die. Printed one at a time in a hand press on special paper, or on glazed card, the engraver's work is seen at its best. Die proofs are normally in black, but are also met with in colour. Die proofs can generally be distinguished by the " plate mark " and the ample margins. Compare PLATE PROOF.

DOMINICAL LABELS.—The small detachable labels below the Belgian stamps of 1893–1914, which bear the instruction in French and Flemish not to deliver on Sunday (Plate 28).

DOUBLE IMPRESSION, DOUBLE PRINT.—Where a sheet of stamps has passed twice through the press, causing the whole to have a double impression. An appearance of double impression is sometimes due to a slurred print, when paper, not being firmly held, has touched the plate before it is in its correct position to receive the proper impression.

DOUBLE PERFORATION.—One or more sides of a stamp may have a double perforation, with space between, or nearly coincident; in the latter case the doubling produces a row of tiny teeth or indentations.

DOUBLE STRIKE.—In typographic printing, moulds are struck from the die in lead, gutta-percha, or wax. If a slight jump or shift occurs in the striking, a thickening or partial doubling of the design may occur, and may be reproduced on the printing plate. It can also occur in recess-printed stamps where the plates have been made by electrotyping.

DOUBLE SURCHARGE.—A true double surcharge should be a clearly double impression of the whole, not just a slurred single impression, which occurs often when surcharging gummed and perforated sheets of stamps, especially in hot climates.

DOUBLE TRANSFER.—A true double transfer is rare in stamp lithography, but apparent or partial doubling of the image on the stone may occur through unskilful handling of the transfers, allowing them to touch the sensitive surface before they are in position; or neglect to clean off a previous image; or through the lines of a design " spreading " on the stone as it is liable to do after wear.

A double transfer in steel-plate printing is referred to as a RE-ENTRY.

DROP LETTER (U.S.).—A letter to be delivered from the office where posted.

DUTY PLATE.—Many modern stamps are printed from two plates, one being the same (the KEY PLATE) for all values; the other, differing for each denomination, is the DUTY PLATE (Plate 29).

ELECTRO, ELECTROTYPE.—A duplicate of the working die, made by galvanic deposit of copper in a mould (matrice) taken from the die. A stamp plate may consist of a number of separate electros clamped together, or the copper shell may be grown in a group of moulds to form a plate.

EMBOSSED PRINTING.—Printing in high relief, with or without colour. See Chapter XV.

ENCASED STAMPS.—Postage stamps wholly or partly covered with celluloid or metal serving as substitutes for small coinage (Plate 28).

EN ÉPARGNE.—The French term for the method of engraving in relief for typographical printing.

ENGINE TURNED.—Intricate traceries forming background patterns for stamps are engraved by means of a rose-engine or geometrical lathe.

ENGRAVED.—Stamps are commonly described as engraved to indicate that they are " line-engraved," i.e. printed from plates engraved in recess. The word has a wider application in printing, as dies for typographical and other forms of printing are engraved.

ENGRAVING ON STONE.—A process rarely, but historically used for stamps, in which the design is cut by a diamond point through a gum film on the stone's surface. A greasy lithographic ink is dabbed into the exposed lines, and is held by the stone. For printing from the finished stone a dabber is used instead of an ink roller, the surface of the stone being kept wet so that the ink is left only where the design is, and the impression is then made on paper. Among the few instances of stamps produced in this way are the first stamp of New Caledonia, 1860, and the locally made Trinidad, 1852–60.

ENTER, ENTRY.—An image transferred by a roller die to its position on a steel plate is said to be " entered." When the plate is fully entered with the required number of images, a proof impression may show one or more entries have not been rolled in deeply enough, so these positions are subjected to a further application of the roller die, called a " fresh entry." After considerable wear in the press, a plate may have some or all of its images " re-entered " to give the plate a renewed lease of use. There is nothing in these successive enterings *except* where the second entry does not exactly coincide with the first. A slight deviation in any direction may cause a partial duplication of lines, which is visible in the printed stamp, and such a variety is styled a RE-ENTRY.

ENTIRE.—Collectors of stamped postal stationery preserve the complete envelopes, post cards, wrappers, etc., as " entires "; some, however, only preserve the stamps from them as CUT-OUTS (which see). Adhesive stamps preserved " on entire " are on their original cover or letter.

ERROR.—A stamp which has been issued with some accidental but marked incorrect deviation from the normal. The error may lie in the design, inscription, colour, paper, watermark, surcharge, etc. The term should not be applied to freaks of " printers' waste," of which leakages occur. Slight deviations from the normal come under the heading VARIETIES (which see).

ESSAY.—A proposed stamp or design which has been rejected, or not adopted, or which, if adopted, has been modified in some particular before issue. In a broader sense the French use the term *essai* for proofs and colour-trials, using the word *projet* for the English " essay " (Plate 28).

EXERCISE BOOK PAPER.—Ruled with blue lines, e.g. Latvia, 1919.

EXPERT, EXPERTISED.—In cases of doubt as to genuineness, stamps can be submitted to an expert, or, better, to a committee of experts, who " expertise " stamps for fees, the scale of which should be consulted before submitting stamps for opinion. In buying rare and expensive stamps it is the custom to buy on the certificate of the Expert Committee of the Royal Philatelic Society, the certificate bearing a photograph of the actual specimen expertised.

EXTENDED MARGIN.—See MARGINS.

FACE.—The front or design side of a stamp.

FACE VALUE.—The denomination or value stated in words or figures on a stamp.

FACSIMILE.—An imitation, akin to a forgery, but sometimes marketed with an overprint denoting its character, e.g. Facsimile, Falsch, or with the Japanese *San-ko*.

FAKE.—A genuine stamp that has been tampered with fraudulently to increase its supposed value to collectors. A normal stamp cunningly altered to represent an " error " or " variety." A letter or cover to which a stamp has been added to make it appear as if on original cover.

FAUX POUR SERVIR.—Forgeries which have passed in the post

or have been made with intent to defraud the post. See Chapter XVIII.

FIRST-DAY COVER.—A stamp used on the first day of its issue and retained on its envelope as evidence of first-day posting.

FIRST FLIGHT.—In aero-philately special attention is given to cards and covers carried on the first flights, whether experimental pioneer efforts or the first flight in either direction on an organised air-mail route.

FISCAL.—A stamp used for revenue purposes other than postage. F.C. is a commonly used contraction to denote that a stamp has a fiscal cancellation, as distinct from a postmark (Plate 28).

FISCAL PHILATELY.—Fiscal and fiscally used stamps are not generally acceptable to collectors of postage stamps. There are collectors in most countries who collect and study fiscal as distinct from postage stamps.

FLAT-PLATE PRINT.—In U.S. stamps identical in design, colour and denomination have been printed on flat-bed and on rotary presses; they are distinguished as flat-plate prints and rotary prints.

FLAW.—A damage to a printing plate or stone may cause a reproduction of the flaw in the printed sheet. Such flaws when constant in an edition or a succession of printings are useful aids in expert work and in PLATING (which see). Such a flaw noticed in the printing works is more or less skilfully corrected by a RETOUCH (which see).

FLOWN COVER, ETC.—An envelope, letter, card, pigeongram, etc., bearing evidence of having been transported by air.

FORGERY.—A counterfeited imitation of a stamp, a surcharge, or a postmark, made to deceive either postal employees or collectors, or both. Compare BOGUS, FACSIMILE, FAKE, and see Chapter XVIII.

FRANK.—In early times Court or Government officials and other privileged persons were allowed to send correspondence free, under cover of their personal " frank," usually their signature in the lower left corner of the address side of the letter.

FREE STAMPS.—See PRIVILEGE STAMPS.

FUGITIVE COLOURS.—Stamps printed in " singly fugitive " inks afford a protection against the removal of postmarks. " Doubly fugitive " inks afford an extra precaution against the removal of writing ink used for pen cancellations.

G. C. PAPER.—See GRANDE CONSOMMATION.

GENERAL COLLECTION.—A collection formed on broad lines, embracing a wide area or group of countries, without specialisation.

GOVERNMENT IMITATIONS.—See OFFICIAL IMITATIONS.

G.P.O., G.PR.O.—Abbreviations for: General Post Office, Government Printing Office.

GRANDE CONSOMMATION, PAPIERS DE.—To economise paper stock during the 1914–18 war, paper of poor quality was used for the manufacture of French and French colonial stamps. Introduced late in 1916, sheet margins bore the initials G.C., and postmasters were advised to use extra care in handling. The papers varied in tone and quality, the commonest being a greyish newsprint recognisable in the stamps at a glance, but others of better quality, white and cream, are not easily distinguishable unless with " G.C." margin.

GRANITE PAPER.—A paper containing small unbleached fibres easily visible on the back of a stamp. Switzerland has used such paper extensively for stamps since 1882, and Japan from 1922 to 1938.

GRILLE.—A plain rectangular embossing on some early United States and Peruvian stamps. It was effected by rolling cylinders with pyramidal bosses over the stamps to break the fibres in the paper, so that the cancelling ink would get into the paper and so be ineradicable (Plate 28).

GUIDE DOTS, GUIDE LINES.—Marks used as guides in entering plates or laying down lithographic stones in alignment. They may merge in the stamp image, or be cleaned off before printing. Often they remain to intrigue collectors who find them useful in PLATING (which see).

GUILLOTINE PERFORATION.—A single straight line of perforating punches, perforating one line at a time in one direction; operated on the up-and-down principle of the guillotine.

GUM.—An unused stamp is normally to be preserved with its original gum (O.G.); stamp hinges properly used will preserve the gum intact. An unused stamp which has lost its gum is sometimes, but improperly, regummed; that is, provided with a faked appearance of original gum.

GUM-BREAKERS.—In modern stamp manufacture, the gummed

surface of the paper is broken up into minute sections by being drawn across steel blades set diagonally in various types of machines. The tiny divisions between the gum particles allow for expansion and contraction in varying temperatures, and counteract any tendency to curl. This non-curling gummed paper rarely shows the action of the breakers in British and colonial stamps; but other types of breakers as used in Germany and U.S.A. show a colourless pattern, described in Germany as riffled (*riffelgummierung*).

GUTTERS.—The spaces left between stamps for perforation or cutting apart. The wider margin between panes is a pane margin. If the pane margin be perforated in the centre, the stamp on each side is said to have an extended margin. See MARGINS.

HABILITADO.—The Spanish word for habilitated is used in many surcharges " enabling " a stamp to be used, i.e. giving it legal validity under a new régime, or when recourse is made to old stock to serve during emergency or shortage of current supplies (Plate 29).

HAIR-LINES.—Originally used to describe the fine line crossing the outer angles of the corner blocks of early typographed British stamps (e.g. the "Nine Pence hair-lines "), which were inserted to distinguish impressions from particular plates.

In modern usage, the term covers other fine lines or scratches met with on line-engraved, litho, or photogravure stamps. Where the lines are identifiable as GUIDE LINES (which see), the latter term is the better.

HAND-STAMPED.—A few adhesive postage stamps have been printed direct from the die, held in a handle, and struck in the manner of a postmark or rubber stamp. Many surcharges have been similarly hand-stamped.

The majority of postmarks for all purposes were hand-stamped until the introduction of electrical rotating-machine postmarks.

HARROW PERFORATION.—An uncommon form of perforation in which the punches are set in rectangular form to perforate a full sheet of stamps at one operation, leaving the sheet margins clear of perforation. The method is now obsolete for postage stamps. See Chapter XVI.

HEAD PLATE.—Another name for KEY PLATE (which see).

HINGE.—Stamp hinges are small strips of paper gummed on one side, and used for hinging or mounting stamps in albums. Also commonly called stamp mounts. See Chapter II.

HOLED.—Holes punched out of stamps generally indicate a form of cancellation. Spanish stamps with circular disk punched out have been used on telegrams. Western Australian stamps, with similar holes, were used for official correspondence. The star-shaped punch in Portuguese stamps was used on telegrams, as in Spain. Other stamps have been punched for various purposes, but the foregoing are the most frequently met with (Plate 29).

IMITATIONS OF STAMPS.—See OFFICIAL IMITATIONS.

IMITATIONS OF WATERMARKS.—See WATERMARKS.

IMPERFORATE.—Contraction IMPERF.—A stamp which has not been perforated or rouletted. IMPERF. BETWEEN describes a pair or more stamps lacking the perforation between them, either vertically or horizontally.

The U.S. Post Office offers for sale " unperforated " stamps, but imperforate stamps are meant.

IMPRESSED WATERMARKS.—See WATERMARKS.

IMPRIMATUR (Latin for " let it be printed ").—It was the custom in Great Britain, as each printing plate was completed, and before it was used for the public issue, that a sheet in the correct colour and on the proper paper should be endorsed with the official sanction to print, and these sheets were registered and preserved at Somerset House. The long series of these imprimatur sheets is still in existence, but mutilated; stamps cut from them are in many private collections.

IMPRINT.—The name of printer or place of printing, on margins of stamp sheets; sometimes on the actual stamps beneath the design (Plate 29).

INDIA PAPER.—A thin fine paper, imported chiefly from China, much used by engravers for taking die proofs.

IN INTAGLIO.—Engraving in recess, as in steel-plate or copper-plate engraving, is IN INTAGLIO; it is also applicable to photogravure. It is the opposite to the Italian IN RELIEVO (which see).

IN RELIEVO.—The Italian term for engraving in relief as for typographical printing.

INTERRUPTED PERFORATION.—For stamps in coil form for delivery by automatic machines, the ordinary perforations tend to weaken the paper too much in the cross-direction of the coil. To counteract this Holland removed several of the punches at intervals. These were christened syncopated perforations when first noted by British collectors, but the Dutch philatelists know them as interrupted perforations. In addition to stamps from coils, some sheets of Dutch stamps have been issued showing the peculiarity (Plate 29).

INTERVERTED.—The wrong way round; cart before the horse. As in " double Geneva," cut the wrong way (Plate 29, Stamp 7).

INVERTED.—Turned upside down. Stamps printed in two colours or requiring two printings sometimes have one of the impressions inverted, through the partly printed sheet being turned the wrong way for the second print. In that way most of the INVERTED CENTRES occurred.

INVERTED SURCHARGES occur in much the same way, whether the surcharge is added in a printing press, or by hand-stamp.

INVERTED WATERMARKS may derive from a similar inversion of the paper before printing, but stamps printed for issue in booklet form in Great Britain, etc., are (as to 50 per cent.) printed upside down. Inverted watermarks are not of major interest. See also TÊTE-BÊCHE.

IRREGULAR PERFORATION.—A perforator whose pins or punches do not gauge uniformly throughout its length.

ISSUE.—The word is used in its several dictionary senses, e.g. a stamp is issued or withdrawn from issue; a group or series of stamps is an issue, old or new issue. It may refer to the edition—the issue was 10,000. An ISSUE SHEET is the sheet as supplied to and by the Post Office.

IVORY HEAD.—The blue discoloration of the paper in early British stamps (see BLEUTÉ) produces some curious vagaries best seen from the back, e.g. the Ivory Head, where the head is left white and the surround is blued (Plate 29).

JUBILEE.—The word has come to be used broadly for commemorative stamps, but is preferably reserved for such stamps as mark periods in a reign, e.g. the Silver Jubilee of King George V

(1935), the Diamond Jubilee anniversary of Queen Victoria; or stamps which bear the word "Jubilee" in inscription or overprint. "Jubilee" is a misnomer for the 1887 issue of Great Britain, which was an ordinary issue long in preparation, which happened to materialise in that year.

JUBILEE LINE.—As a protection against the wear of typographical stamp plates at their edges, a rule was added round each pane or plate of most of the British and colonial stamps. It appears as a line of colour on the sheets. It is known to collectors as the "Jubilee line," for no other reason than that it was first adopted in 1887 (Plate 27).

KEYED.—A term used in PLATING (which see) where a pair, strip, or block is found to key-up with a position or variety already identified.

KEY PLATE.—The plate bearing a common design for a series of stamp denominations, or for groups of colonial stamps, but leaving blank spaces for the addition of figures, name, etc., by a second plate, known as the DUTY PLATE (Plate 29).

KEY-STONE.—Lithographic stamps printed in two or more colours are printed from two or more stones. The first stone bears the key design, or outline pattern, repeated to the required number of units. A specially prepared proof from this, on a non-stretching paper, is the key-sheet; on this transfers are laid in correct position for the first colour; the transfers adhere to the stone, leaving the key-sheet free to receive the transfers for the next colour. And so stone after stone is laid down, each in correct register with the rest, to do its part in the colour scheme. The key-stone is not necessarily used in the actual printing.

KNIFE.—The shape of the blank paper cut out to be folded into envelope form is called the knife.

LAID PAPER.—With a texture of lines close together, usually with other lines crossing them wide apart.

LINE-ENGRAVING.—Engraving with incised lines, as in steel- or copper-plate engraving. In philately the expression "line-engraved" is applied to a stamp produced in this way.

LITHOGRAPH, LITHOGRAPHED. Contraction LITHO.—Stamps printed from designs drawn or transferred upon stone, or in modern practice on metal surfaces substituted for lithographic stone. Stamps so printed are smooth to the touch. See Chapter XV.

LOCALS.—Stamps whose franking power is circumscribed, within a town, or district, or limited to a particular route. Where issued by direct Government authority, they are listed in the regular stamp catalogues. The great majority of " local " stamps are, however, of two main divisions: (*a*) sanctioned or permitted by authority, but issued under local or private concerns, and intended to supplement the regular postal service; and (*b*) by private persons or companies conducting posts of their own, independent of, although often supplementing the Government post (Plate 30).

LOGOTYPE.—A piece of type comprising two or more letters or a word, cast in one piece.

MACHINE CANCELLATION.—A postmark and cancelling mark applied by a rotary die driven by electricity; the cancelling portion is often used for publicity or propaganda slogans, or flags.

MAKE-READY.—Before printing from a plate, a proof is taken on an impression sheet from which portions which print too fully are cut away, and others which do not give a clear impression are patched up with portions cut from other sheets. The sheet thus treated is placed on the tympan of the press or on the impression cylinder, and is fixed there, as an *overlay*, to correct the inequalities in the printing surface. It seems finicky work, and is now largely done by mechanical processes. Make-ready is of special importance in typographical stamp printing where the extremely fine lines have to be given their full value, not just on one stamp, but on each of the 100, 240, or more units on a plate.

It serves to produce some philatelic curios, but is more useful to collectors in distinguishing different printings, and the work of different printers.

In addition to the *overlay*, there is often an *underlay* of thicknesses of paper on the under side of a plate.

MANILA PAPER.—A strong, light, coarse paper, usually smooth on one side and rough on the other, commonly used for stamped envelopes and wrappers.

MANUSCRIPT SURCHARGES.—In rare emergencies stamps have had their denominations altered in manuscript, usually (but not always) accompanied by the initials of a postal official.

Margins.—The margins of stamp sheets are of much interest to collectors, for they often bear marks, especially register marks, pointers and numbers, imprints, dates, controls, and other inscriptions, which convey information of use to students. In addition to the outer *sheet margins*, there are often margins between the panes, *pane margins*; the latter when divided by a single line of perforation give us *extended* or *wing margins* (Plate 30). In the pane margins of French and French colonial stamps are found the *millésimes*. The narrow spaces between stamps for the perforations are Gutters (which see).

Warning.—Do not use stamp-edging as a cheap substitute for stamp hinges; it sticks like glue.

Master Plate.—By taking a matrix from a complete stamp plate, duplicates are made for use in the printing press, the original being reserved as a master plate.

Matrix.—A counterpart impression in metal or other material from an original die, and which in its turn is used to produce copies exactly similar to the original die.

Metered Mail, Meter Marks.—Mail franked by postage meter machines, used by private concerns under licence or permit; these machines impress the mark of prepayment on the mail, and automatically record the amount due to the post office.

Millésime.—The figures, large or small, denoting the date of minting coins or printing stamps. In stamps of French manufacture the *millésime*, represented by the last figure of the year, appears in the pane margins, e.g. 9 = 1909, or 1939 (Plate 30).

Mill Sheet.—The sheet as manufactured. See Sheet.

Mint.—An unused stamp in perfect condition, with full gum, is described as " mint." An early term used in America, now obsolete, was " in post office state," but stamps bought at the post office are not necessarily fine enough for a collector. Unused stamps that were *issued* without gum, if otherwise perfect, are still " mint."

Mirror Print.—A rare class of error in which the stamp design is printed in reverse. Examples occur in Turkey's lithographed first issue (1863).

Mixed Perforations.—Sheets of stamps defectively perforated are sometimes patched locally at the back, and reperforated, usually with a different gauge of perforation. An economical measure chiefly associated with New Zealand 1901–07 issues.

MIXTURES.—Stamps collected in quantities from correspondence, sold in bulk to the stamp trade, and parcelled out in smaller lots to collectors hunting for what they may find. Some postal administrations save used stamps off postal dockets or telegrams and sell them in bulk. " Bank mixtures " are supposed to derive from a bank's mail, and " mission mixtures " from the various charity organisations.

MOIRÉ.—A pattern something like " watered silk " was lithographed on the backs of sheets of the Mexico issue of 1872, and on the front surface of certain British Honduras stamps of 1915. Compare BURELE, BURELAGE.

MONSTER.—Dutch for SPECIMEN (which see).

MOULD.—Another name for the matrix.

MOUNTED.—A defective stamp that has had new margins added is said to have been " mounted." This class of fraud is chiefly met with in connection with early stamps of unusual shape which have been spoiled by being CUT TO SHAPE (which see).

MUESTRA.—The Spanish word for " Specimen," overprinted on stamps of Spanish and Latin American countries. See SPECIMEN.

NADRUCK.—Dutch for REPRINT (which see).

NE PAS LIVRER LE DIMANCHE.—See DOMINICAL LABELS.

NEW-ISSUE SERVICE.—A service in which a stamp dealer aided by a network of agents and correspondents in all parts of the world secures early importations or supplies of new stamps, and distributes them to his clients on a subscription basis, or at a fixed percentage over the face value.

NEWSPAPER STAMPS.—Some countries have, or have had, separate stamps for use in posting newspapers, their purpose being sometimes indicated in the inscription; others have been without such superscription, their low denominations sufficiently denoting their use.

NON-CURLING GUMMED PAPER.—See GUM-BREAKERS.

NUMBERS.—In connection with the control and checking of stamps in manufacture and distribution, systems of numeration have a considerable share. Where such numeration appears on the front or back of stamps, or in the margins of panes or sheets they have something to tell the collector. Uruguay stamps of 1882 had figures incorporated into the design, from 1–100, each stamp on the sheet of 100 bearing a different number. In Spain, 1875, framed numbers 1–100 figured on the backs of stamps, and in 1900 multiple numbering machines impressed unframed rotation numbers on the back of every stamp, each sheet of 100 receiving a new number starting from 000,001 (Plate 30). See also CONTROL, CURRENT NUMBER, CYLINDER NUMBER, PLATE NUMBER, ROTATION NUMBER.

OBLITERATION.—Any mark used to cancel a stamp; and especially if it has been applied with too much zeal.

OBSOLETE.—Stamps or series of stamps no longer in circulation or use are described as obsolete.

ODONTOMÈTRE.—The name by which the pioneer collector, Dr. Legrand, introduced his invention of the PERFORATION GAUGE (which see). The name is current in French philately.

OFFICIAL.—Adhesive stamps of all kinds prepared for the franking of correspondence of Government departments are classed under the general heading of " Official Stamps," although they may have other local appellations, e.g. Departmentals, Service Stamps, etc.

OFFICIAL IMITATIONS.—Stamps imitated by authority to provide specimens for exhibition or sale, after the original dies, plates, or watermarked paper were no longer available. See Chapter XVII.

OFFICIALLY SEALED, OFFICIAL SEALS.—Although listed in a few cases in stamp catalogues, labels used for sealing mail found open in the post, or opened in the Returned Letter Office, are not postage stamps.

OFFSET.—The set-off of ink from one printed sheet to another when wet. Now more conveniently called a SET-OFF, not to be confused with OFFSET PROCESSES.

OFFSET PROCESSES OF PRINTING.—In which specially prepared plates, chiefly lithographic, are printed on to a rubber-blanketed cylinder, which then offsets the impression on to paper. See Chapter XV.

OPENED UP.—A die which is worn, or is not yielding perfect replicas for printing, is sometimes opened up; it or a replica is gone over by a skilled engraver, who deepens incised parts, and with other refinements improves the reproductive quality of the die. The resulting stamps may show more or less distinct differences, as in the Humphrys' retouch of the " old original " Queen's-head die of Great Britain (line-engraved) and the first printings of the $\frac{1}{2}d$. and $1d$. King George V stamps (typographed); Dies 1 and 2 of the Queen's-head general colonial key plates are well-known typographical examples of " opening up."

ORIGINAL.—A genuine stamp as it was issued or used, as compared with a REISSUE, or as opposed to a REPRINT. See also COVER, DIE, GUM.

OVERLAY.—The patched-up impression sheet with varying thicknesses of paper to bring up the full effect of a printing plate is an *overlay*, as distinguished from an *underlay*, which latter consists of patching thicknesses of paper under the type, block, or plate. See MAKE-READY.

OVERPRINT.—Any device or inscription printed upon a stamp additional to its original design.

OVERPRINT PLATE.—An official printing term for a DUTY PLATE (which see).

PACKET, PACKET-BOAT.—In post office use in addition to the familiar sense of a small parcel, packet may refer to a mail dispatched to or received from abroad by packet-boat, i.e. a mail-carrying vessel plying at regular intervals.

PAIR.—A couple of stamps which have not been separated. Unless qualified as a *vertical pair* $\substack{\square \\ \square}$, a horizontal pair $\square\square$ is generally implied. See SE TENANT.

PANE.—A rectangular division of a sheet of stamps, divided by pane margins into sections for convenience in selling and accounting. The early line-engraved British stamps were set solid, 240, or 480; but with the adoption of higher denominations typographed, the sheets were arranged in from two up to twelve panes. These sheets, while printed in sheets of 240, were in most cases divided before issue to the post offices. British colonial stamps in key-plate designs were printed 240 up in four panes of sixty, or 120 up in two panes, or for small editions in sheets of sixty. Modern English low-value stamps, long issued in sheets of two panes, are now printed paneless, saving an appreciable amount of paper.

PANELESS.—A sheet of stamps set in a single group without division into panes.

PANTOGRAPH.—The principle of this instrument in its simple form for copying a drawing on the same or an enlarged or reduced scale is commonly known. The instrument has been much used in engraving, and probably many of the early hand-engraved stamps, like the Nevis, the Sydney Views, etc., owe something to its use. In large establishments it has been, and still is, used for engraving through an etching ground, denominations on an undenominated plate, marginal inscriptions, etc. A brass model of the figure or lettering required serves as a guide to the tracer which controls the engraving point; the latter repeats the design on the etching ground.

PANTOGRAPH VARIETIES.—Slight errors or omissions in tracing the model, whether in the single or multiple pantograph, are transmitted to the stamps.

Virgin Islands. Incomplete letters due to small omissions in pantograph work.

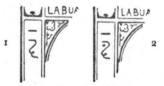

(1) Labuan. Dot omitted from Malay character shown in (2).

PAPER of one kind or another is an essential part of every adhesive postage stamp. The subject is treated as a whole in Chapter XVI.

PAPILLONS.—Flimsies bearing messages sent by free balloons out of Metz in 1870. See BALLON NON MONTÉ.

PAQUEBOT.—French word for PACKET-BOAT (which see) in international use in postmarks on sea-borne letters, and found on stamps.

PARAPH.—The flourish ending a signature, or signed initials. Printed paraphs appear on stamps of Cuba used in Porto Rico (Plate 30).

PELLICULES.—Thin, sensitised films on which messages were copied by photo-micrography for conveyance by pigeon post during the siege of Paris, 1870-71. On arrival, they were projected on to a lantern screen, transcribed, and the messages delivered.

PELURE PAPER.—A crisp, thin, hard paper; the description is commonly given to varieties of stamps on any paper that is very thin and hard.

PEN-CANCELLED.—Any cancellation made with pen and writing ink. Postage stamps cancelled in writing have in most cases been used for fiscal purposes. Some countries issued their earliest stamps without providing the postmasters with instructions or means for cancelling them; such stamps were left uncancelled, or cancelled with pen or pencil. To find a postmark on such a stamp would be a matter for suspicion.

PERCÉ.—French for pierced, used by French philatelists in the sense of ROULETTED (which see).

PERFORATION.—The method now almost universal for rendering stamps easily detachable from each other. It is contrived by machines provided with punches, which work through a guide plate into a bed plate. The effect is to punch clean holes, from which tiny disks fall away like confetti. It is distinct from ROULETTING, which cuts or pricks the paper. See Chapter XVI.

PERFORATION GAUGE.—The handy scale of card, celluloid, or metal furnished with graduated series of dots and lines in a column 2 centimetres wide, for use in measuring perforations and roulettes. The gauge or measure is reckoned in terms of the number of holes or cuts formed in the standard length of 2 centimetres. The accessory's use is explained in Chapter II.

PERMITS.—See METERED MAIL.

PHILATELY.—The name given to the collection and study of stamps. The " a " is pronounced as in man, or fashion, and the " e " as in tell, the whole as fil-at-eli. PHILATELIC.—Relating to philately. PHILATELIST.— A stamp collector.

PIGEONGRAM.—A flimsy message flown by pigeon post.

PILLARS, PILLAR BLOCKS.—The devices printed in broad margins of watermarked paper (e.g. between panes) to prevent it from being used for counterfeiting (Plate 31).

PIN-PERFORATION.—One of the inconsistencies of philatelic terminology. It is actually a roulette, being made by pin-points which pierce but do not perforate the paper.

PIQUÉ, PIQUAGE.—French synonyms for the more general DENTELÉ, DENTELURE, i.e. perforated, perforation.

PLATE.—A term used broadly to describe the printing surface which receives ink and makes the impression, covering not only a metal plate with stamp images engraved upon it, but also a group of clichés locked together, a *forme* of printers' type used for printing stamps, a lithographic stone, or even a cylinder. Most plates were flat until the modern developments of rotary processes. *Curved plates* are engraved flat and bent into half-circular shape, two such plates meeting to form a cylinder.

PLATE NUMBER.—In well-conducted printeries strict control and record are kept of every plate made. There are various systems of numbering them, and where these are engraved on the plate they appear on the printed sheet. There was for many years in Great Britain a dual system of numbering. Every plate for a particular denomination was given a consecutive number, which appears on the sheet margin, and in some cases in small figures on every stamp in the sheet. British specialists reserve the term " plate number " for such. The collateral system was the CURRENT NUMBER (which see).

Since the Bureau of Engraving and Printing (Washington, D.C.) took over the printing of U.S. stamps in 1894, upwards of 23,000 stamp plates have been made, numbered consecutively in the margins, and actual sheets of nearly all are preserved in the archives of the Bureau.

PLATE PROOF.—Proofs printed from a plate, as distinct from a die, show no more margin than the gutters between the stamps on the sheet allow; outside positions, however, may have the sheet margin at one or two sides only. Compare DIE PROOF.

PLATING.—A fascinating exercise, much favoured by specialists, of trying to reassemble sheets of stamps from singles, pairs, strips, and blocks, allotting each to its position on the original.

Intensified study by collectors has shown that while all the stamps on one sheet are in a sense identical, many of them present small clues which permit individual units to be identified and so "plated." Some remarkable results have been achieved from co-ordinated efforts to reconstruct a plate, even when the size or constitution of the plate has not been known. Where material is accessible in multiples, pairs, etc., the patience of the jig-saw puzzler and the observation of a sleuth help one to key pairs and blocks.

POCHETTES.—Transparent glassine envelopes of stamp sizes, sometimes used to protect stamps, and to preserve them " mint."

POSTAL FISCAL.—A stamp primarily issued for fiscal purposes which has been duly authorised for postal use.

POSTAL UNION.—See UNIVERSAL POSTAL UNION.

POSTMARK.—Any mark stamped on mail by postal officials or agents, i.e. for any postal purpose. It may be a simple cancellation for the postage stamp or a date mark, an indication of route, an instruction, etc. As a general practice the postmark of the office of dispatch is applied on the front (or stamp) side of a letter, and the office of arrival mark on the back.

POSTMARKED TO ORDER.—See CANCELLED TO ORDER.

POSTMASTERS' STAMPS, POSTMASTERS' PROVISIONALS.—Stamps issued by postmasters on their own responsibility prior to the adoption of the stamp system by the U.S. Government (1845-47); also stamps so issued by postmasters in the Confederate States during the Civil War (1861–65). The postmaster of Hamilton, Bermuda, issued home-made 1d. stamps in 1848 (Plate 31).

PRE-CANCEL, PRE-CANCELLATION.—The system whereby large mailing concerns in U.S., Canada, and some European countries are supplied with stamps already cancelled, to save time and labour in the Post Office. The system has been so widely used in America that consignments of stamps are printed and pre-cancelled at the Bureau of Engraving and Printing, and delivered thus, the cancellation usually consisting of the town name (Plate 31).

PREMIÈRES GRAVURES.—First impressions. The expression is chiefly used to describe the rare United States first (or August) issue of 1861, the plates for which were subjected to minor improvements before the fuller issue, known as the September

1861 series. The term is also applied to fine early impressions from line-engraved plates, in particular those which were hand-engraved on copper.

PREPARED FOR USE BUT NEVER ISSUED.—A few stamps which were never put into circulation in the post are included in the catalogues on account of their special interest, e.g. Great Britain 1d. black with letters VR in top corners, India ½ anna vermilion, 1854, Cape of Good Hope 1d. triangular with Crown CC watermark, etc.

PRE-STAMP COVERS.—Letters or covers posted in any country prior to the adoption by that country of the postage-stamp system.

PRINTERS' WASTE.—In preparing plates and working up for colour, in the printery, much paper is used and thrown aside as waste. In properly regulated works it is scrupulously destroyed. From other factories much of this waste leaks out and is sometimes imposed upon collectors as rare freaks of double, treble, etc., impressions; printed both sides; on coloured papers other than those appropriate to the issued stamps (Plate 31).

PRINTING.—The different methods of printing postage stamps are described in Chapter XV.

PRINTINGS.—A supply of stamps of one or several denominations printed at one period is described as a printing; further supplies printed from time to time of the same stamps constitute fresh printings, and the stamps, when distinguishable by colour or shade, or other details, are referred to as of the first, second, third printing. The term is often shortened to " print," as in First Athens print; London print, etc.

PRIVATE PERFORATIONS—ROULETTES.—Perforations or roulettes made by individuals or companies for their own convenience, in most cases before perforation became general for stamps. See also AUTOMATIC PERFORATION.

PRIVILEGE STAMPS.—A limited class of stamps supplied to, or permitted to be used by, individuals or institutions granted privileges in the matter of free postage, e.g. Portugal, Royal Geographical Society; Spain, Members of Parliament (Plate 31).

PROOF.—An impression, usually in black, from the die plate or stone, taken in order to see if the design and other details have been properly engraved or reproduced. Compare COLOUR TRIALS.

PROVISIONALS.—Temporary makeshifts created when definite stamps are lacking, e.g. when a denomination has run out of stock, or when a new one is required but has not yet been supplied. The most general expedient is to surcharge other stamps which are in stock.

Q.H.—The initials commonly used for " Queen's Head," or " Queen's Heads " (as applied to most British and colonial issues of the Victorian era). Similar contractions are K.H. (King's Head), now more particularly K.E. (King Edward VII) and K.G.V and K.G.VI.

QUADRILLÉ.—In 1892 the 15 centimes stamp of France, and subsequently pictorial stamps of Obock and Djibouti, were printed on plain white paper, which was given a ground print of uncoloured varnish forming a quadrillé pattern, which at first glance looks like, and is commonly mistaken for, a watermark. It served as a protective ground print.

Very few instances occur of stamps being printed on paper *watermarked* with small squares and rectangles, and these are chiefly obscure and rare local productions.

Leaves, sheets, cards, etc., used for stamp albums or display are commonly printed with a feint quadrillé pattern as an aid. See Chapter IV.

QUARTZ LAMP.—A lamp generating violet rays, much used by experts for detecting alterations or repairs to stamps. A philatelic accessory de luxe. See Chapter XVIII.

RARE (R).—A stamp or a variety of a stamp, or a condition in which a stamp is uncommon. Degrees of rarity are sometimes expressed by R, RR, RRR, but rarity is comparative and indefinite. The limit is reached in the few " unique " stamps of which only *single* examples are known.

RECESS PLATE, RECESS PRINTING.—A plate engraved with lines incised; printing from such plates. See LINE-ENGRAVING.

RECONSTRUCTION.—Another term for PLATING (which see), but platers prefer the shorter word.

RECUT, RE-ENGRAVED.—When a die or plate has been considerably re-engraved, sometimes changing it in important details, it is said to be recut or re-engraved. Compare RETOUCH.

REDRAWN.—A design already in use, but found not wholly satisfactory in printing, or by reason of some faulty detail, is redrawn and a new die engraved. A familiar example is the Rights of Man design of France, issued in 1900, and redrawn in 1902.

RE-ENTRY.—See ENTRY.

REGISTER MARKS.—Most commonly crosses + printed in the sheet margins, and in many cases pricked with point holes during printing. Their purpose is to secure register (i.e. exact adjustment) with the second impression (if any), and to obtain accurate register of the perforations.

REISSUE.—A stamp or series of stamps brought back into use after it has been superseded and out of use. It sometimes implies a new issue.

RELIEVO.—See IN RELIEVO.

REMAINDERS.—Stamps remaining in stock or returned to stock when an issue is superseded are at times destroyed, but some countries have dumped them on the stamp market, sometimes obligingly cancelling them (see CANCELLED TO ORDER). There is nothing to indicate remainders if not cancelled, the stamps being originals; the dumping causes some to be cheaper unused than used. In economical Great Britain, stock of one issue is allowed to become exhausted before a new issue is put into full general circulation. See Chapter XVII.

REP.—Wove paper that has been milled between ridged instead of smooth rollers.

REPRINT.—An impression taken from an original plate or stone of stamps that have gone out of use, or from new plates or stones derived from the original die. Where neither die nor plate has been available and new ones are engraved on Government authority, they are Government, or OFFICIAL IMITATIONS (which see). Private reprints are those made by persons or firms who have acquired dies, plates, and other printing material which would have been better destroyed.

RESET.—Stamps or surcharges printed from printers' type are often required to be reset when further supplies are required. See SETTING.

RETOUCH.—An impression from a die, plate, or other printing surface which has been retouched to correct or remove a defect or to strengthen lines or parts that are printing weakly. The retouch may occur before any stamps are printed, or at a later stage after wear. In the latter case the student may trace specimens of a particular stamp before it has been retouched, and after (Plate 31).

REVERSED.—Stamps printed with their designs reversed are few (see MIRROR PRINTS); watermarks are frequently found reversed, owing to the paper being turned. Collectors should avoid using the word reversed when they mean INVERTED (which see).

RIBBED PAPER.—One side is smooth and the other is in alternate furrows and ridges; the paper is thinner in the furrows than in the ridges.

ROCKED, INSUFFICIENTLY.—An image on a steel plate, if the transfer roller has not been sufficiently rocked, may lack the outer frame lines or ornaments at top or bottom if rocked vertically, or at the sides if rocked laterally. Alternatively, such external lines may be present, but weak.

ROLL OF STAMPS.—See COILS.

ROLLER DIE.—The reversed image of the flat original die, taken up on the Transfer Roller, to be retransferred to the flat steel plate. See TRANSFER ROLLER.

ROSACE.—The little embossed or impressed device formerly found on the loose flap of early manufactured envelopes in imitation of the old-fashioned wafer used in sealing. Also called the TRESSE.

ROTARY PERFORATION.—In rotary perforating the punches are set on metal wheels which work through the paper into corresponding wheels with holes drilled in them. A set of such wheeled punches will perforate all the gutters in a sheet of stamps in one direction, and the sheet has to be passed through the machine a second time to obtain the perforation in the other direction. The effect at the junction of the perforated lines is as in single-line perforation (see page 133).

ROTARY PRINTING.—The chief methods used in modern stamp printing have been adapted to comparatively rapid printing on long webs of paper, from cylinders instead of flat plates. Where stamps of like design have been produced by both methods, the stamps are distinguished as " Flat-plate print " and " Rotary print " respectively.

ROTATION NUMBER.—The consecutive number applied as a

check on the sheets of stamp paper. In some cases the sheets of paper are issued to the printer already numbered. In flat sheets the number may be done by a small hand-operated numbering machine, or by a numbering appliance attached to the printing press. In rotary printing the numbering is done in the press at every revolution of the cylinder.

ROULETTE, ROULETTING.—The purpose of the roulette is to render stamps easily detachable from each other, as in PERFORATION. In rouletting, the pins, cuts, or rules only pierce or stab the paper, without punching it out. The word derives from the toothed wheels used by hand to make the incisions, but the term is retained for stamps pierced or cut (but not punched) by raised printers' rules in the press, or by means akin to the domestic sewing-machine (Plate 31).

ROW.—The horizontal line of the sheet is the *row*, as distinct from the vertical *column*.

RULED PAPER.—As used for manuscript paper, exercise-book paper, etc.; printed with lines for guidance in writing.

SAGGIO.—Italian for SPECIMEN.

SAMPLE.—As an overprint it is the equivalent of SPECIMEN (which see).

SCREEN.—In half-tone typographical printing, and in mechanical photogravure, the image is obtained through a fine screen of crossed lines, which split up the image on the printing plate or cylinder to produce variations in tone. The divisions in the printed impressions blend, but close inspection shows that the stamp picture is split up by tiny intersections. The distinguishing characteristics of the screens in the two processes mentioned are set out in Chapter XV.

SEA POST.—Modern stamps of one country bearing the postmark of another country commonly derive from letters posted at sea, i.e. on ships. In earlier times sea postage was the subject of a separate charge, paid to captains of vessels, or the owners' agents. The " Porte de Mar " stamps of Mexico, 1875, represented sea postage to be accounted for, before Mexico joined the Postal Union.

SEEBECKS.—The late Mr. N. F. Seebeck, a stamp collector who was also representative of a Bank Note Company, entered into contracts with South and Central American Governments to print their postage-stamp requirements without charge, but stipulating that a new issue was to be made each year, the remainders of the previous series to be delivered to him, and himself reserving the right to use the old plates for printing as many more stamps as he found a sale for among collectors. Philatelists resented the extraordinary terms of the Seebeck contracts, and their protests were so effective that the contracts were not renewed (1889–99).

SE TENANT.—A French expression, for which there is no concise English term, meaning holding together or not separated. It is conveniently used to describe two different stamps or two varieties of the stamp, in an unseparated pair. An error in conjunction with a normal stamp in a pair is so described. Occasionally two different denominations may be met with *se tenant* (Plate 32).

SET-OFF.—The accidental transfer of undried ink from one surface to another. Occasionally stamps are met with in which a strong set-off on the back gives a complete reversed image of the design, as in a mirror print. A set-off is of minor consequence in philately, but see BOTH SIDES (Plate 32).

SETTING.—A composition of printers' type for a stamp or a surcharge, even if " kept standing," may need some resetting if it be required to print further supplies. Often the whole may have to be set. The study, including the reconstruction or plating of successive settings, is of particular value in expertising such stamps and surcharges.

SHEET.—Stamps are printed in sheets of from one stamp to several hundreds. They are commonly printed in sheets of larger size than those issued to the public. Sheets of paper as delivered from the paper mill are known as *mill sheets*; these may be cut down before printing, and the *printers' sheet* is often cut down again to become the *post office* or *issue sheet*.

The expression *miniature sheet* formerly referred to small reconstructions of British typographed stamps showing in much-reduced form the arrangement of stamps and borders. In modern usage the term covers the plethora of little sheets or blocks so printed for commemorative, souvenir, and speculative purposes.

SHEET NUMBER.—See ROTATION NUMBER.

SHIP LETTER.—In the eighteenth century letters departing, or arriving, from overseas began to be marked with cachets showing port of arrival, e.g. SHIP LETTER (or LRE), Portsmouth, etc.

SILK-THREAD PAPER.—See DICKINSON PAPER.

SILURIAN.—See GRANITE PAPER.

SLOGAN POSTMARKS.—See MACHINE CANCELLATION.

SPANDREL.—The irregular triangular space between a circle, oval, or curve, and the rectangular frame enclosing it.

SPECIALISE, SPECIALISM.—The concentration of collecting interest on a limited field.

SPECIMEN STAMPS.—Stamps overprinted with the word " Specimen " are used for a variety of purposes (see CANCELLATION), but most extensively for distribution through the International Bureau of the Universal Postal Union, to postal administrations of all countries to show what stamps have been issued and are valid in other countries. " Specimen " is in widely general use for this purpose; " Sample " is rarely met with, but equivalents in other languages are: " Malli " (Finnish), " Muestra " (Spanish), " Saggio " (Italian), " Monster " (Dutch) (Plate 32).

SPECULATIVE ISSUES.—Those made and issued with more anticipation of sales on the stamp market than for use in the postal service.

SPLIT STAMPS.—A colloquial expression for stamps which have been divided in two, three, or four pieces for use in the post in those proportions of their face value (Plate 32). Halves of stamps so used are commonly styled BISECTS, or BISECTED STAMPS (which see).

STAMP CURRENCY.—Stamps used in lieu of money during war or other emergency causing shortage of subsidiary coinage. Sometimes expressly printed for such use; sometimes encased (Plate 32). See ENCASED STAMPS.

STEREOTYPE, STEREO.—A reproduction of a die or setting of type, cast in type-metal from a papier-mâché or a plaster mould.

STITCH WATERMARK.—Little met with among British stamp papers, but encountered in American stamps, this is not a true WATERMARK (which see), but is formed by wire stitches made in joining or repairing the " endless " wirecloth.

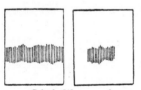

Stitch Watermarks

It generally appears as a group of stitches.

STRIP.—Three or more stamps unsevered in a single row or column; e.g. horizontal strip, or vertical strip.

SUNDAY LABELS.—See DOMINICAL LABELS.

SURCHARGE.—A term originally introduced from France to denote a printed addition to a completed stamp; in fact, an overprint, but nowadays commonly confined to an overprint altering the face value.

SURFACE-COLOURED.—Usually white papers, coated on the printing side with colour. See also WHITE BACKS.

SURFACE PRINTING, SURFACE PRINTED.—Philatelists commonly use these words for TYPOGRAPHY, TYPOGRAPHED (which see). The terms are correct, but liable to confusion.

TAILLE DOUCE.—See LINE-ENGRAVING.

TÊTE-BÊCHE, lit. head to foot.—When, by the inversion of one or more clichés or transfers, a sheet of stamps contains stamps inverted in relation to their neighbours, a normal and inverted stamp unsevered form a TÊTE-BÊCHE pair. The two stamps may form a horizontal or vertical TÊTE-BÊCHE pair, or the TÊTE-BÊCHE condition may form part of a strip or block. Where one stamp of a pair is sideways, but not inverted, it is not TÊTE-BÊCHE, but would be described as " pair, one stamp sideways" (Plate 32).

THINNED.—Stamps carelessly removed from envelopes or back paper, or from which hinges have been removed, are liable to lose a part of the surface of the paper at the back.

TIED.—A stamp is said to be tied, or well tied, on a letter, cover, or a piece of cover when the postmark extends neatly over part of the stamp and the adjacent part of the cover. The significance of the expression lies in distinguishing a genuine cover from one that has been faked; and especially in the case of bisected stamps, where it is desirable to have the postmark overlapping the line of bisection.

TONED.—Paper with a very slight buff tint. The word is also used to distinguish the gum on different printings of an issue with " white gum " or " toned gum."

TRANSFER.—In lithography the design is multiplied by taking impressions in special ink on prepared transfer paper and then laying them down singly or in multiples to produce the working stone. The impressions on transfer paper are *transfers*, and in philately the term is also used to denote the images after they have been transferred to the stone.

TRANSFER ROLLER.—The cylindrical steel roller which takes up an impression from a flat steel die and transfers many impressions of it on to the steel plate in line-engraving. More rarely used for transferring a relief die to a plate for typographical printing. The periphery of the roller is as wide as the stamp, and may bear several raised images of the same or other original dies. The image on the TRANSFER ROLLER is described as the ROLLER DIE.

TRESSE.—See ROSACE.

TYPE.—A representative design, common to an issue or a series or group of issues, e.g. " Peace and Commerce type " (France), " Colonial key-plate type," etc. Used also as referring to the design as distinguished from VARIETIES, or deviations from it.

TYPE, TYPE-SET.—The movable types used by printers have been used in great variety for the composition of the actual designs of stamps and of overprints and surcharges, and in precancellation. Printers have names for the different styles, sizes, etc. of type.

A type-set stamp is one wholly set in printers' type, which includes printers' ornaments and rules. Early British Guianas, Hawaiian Islands, are good examples. See also SETTING.

TYPOGRAPHY.—Originally the art of printing from movable types, it now includes printing from plates or cylinders whereon the designs are in relief, the raised lines receiving the ink and giving off the impression. In typography the raised printing lines cause a slight indentation of the paper. Philatelists also use the expression " surface-printing " (e.g. the surface-printed stamps of Great Britain) as synonymous with TYPOGRAPHY, TYPOGRAPHED (see Chapter IX). Equivalents: EN ÉPARGNE; IN RELIEVO.

ULTRA-VIOLET LAMP.—See QUARTZ LAMP.

UNDERLAY.—In making ready a plate for printing, it may require underlay (i.e. on the back of the plate) as well as an OVERLAY (which see).

UNIVERSAL POSTAL UNION.—Agreements between the Postal Administrations of adjacent or political groups have resulted in the formation of limited Postal Unions from early times (e.g. the German-Austrian Postal Union, formed 1850). The Universal Postal Union, founded in 1874, now embraces every country having an organised postal service, and its conventions regulate international relations between postal administrations of the world. Abbreviation: U.P.U.

UNIVERSAL POSTAL UNION COLOURS.—At the Washington Convention of the Universal Postal Union, 1898, it was recommended that the postage stamps of all nations in those denominations denoting the three standard units of postage rates in the international service should be of uniform colours. The rates are on a gold basis, and the respective colours allotted to them were: 5 centimes green, 10 centimes red, and 25 centimes blue. The recommendation was confirmed at the Rome Convention of 1906 and thereafter became effective in most countries. Disruption of currencies and postage rates after the first World War has since interfered with complete uniformity in this respect.

UNUSED.—A stamp that has not been used, and in philatelic parlance implying one that has not been abused. In perfect state the unused stamp may be described as *mint*, or with full *original gum* (O.G.).

USED.—A stamp that has been used, and generally implying *used postally*, unless specifically stated to have been *fiscally used* or having telegraph cancellation.

USED ABROAD.—Before certain countries and colonies had postage stamps of their own, British post offices or postal agencies were set up in them, where British stamps could be obtained and used. They were the contemporary stamps of Great Britain, and their extra-territorial use can only be distinguished by the postmarks. The stamps of France, U.S.A., and other countries are also met with *used abroad*.

VALUE.—See CATALOGUE VALUE; FACE VALUE; DENOMINATION.

VALUE TABLET.—The rectangular, curved or oval space in a stamp design containing words or figures denoting the face value.

VARIETY.—Used in a number of its dictionary meanings; a variety packet consists of stamps which are all different; but more particularly a stamp which exhibits some small variation from the normal stamp in any detail of its composition. An important or prominent variety may be an error worthy of being so classified, but minor variations, even if constituting mistakes, are varieties rather than ERRORS (which see). In PLATING (which see) the stamps on a sheet are all of the same *type*, but are reconstructed by finding small differences which are minor *varieties*, most of them too small to be of consequence except in plating or to advanced specialists.

VARNISH LINES.—Diagonal lines or bars of uncoloured shiny varnish were used by Austria as a protective ground print. The quadrillé pattern on certain French stamps was printed in colourless varnish, but not shiny. See also QUADRILLÉ, and CHALK LINES.

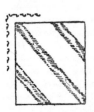

VIGNETTE.—The central or otherwise-placed portrait, picture view, as distinct from its frame. In stamps printed in two operations, the vignette plate is akin to the key plate, the complementary plate is the frame plate.

WATERMARK.—The devices, letters, or words formed in paper during its manufacture, and made by metal " bits " sewn on the mould in hand-made paper; or on the dandy roll in machine-made paper. See Chapter XVI.

WATERMARKS, IMITATIONS OF.—Stamps printed on paper without watermark are sometimes given an impressed or printed device on the back as a substitute for a true watermark. Examples: Russia, 1858 (impressed without colour), New Zealand, 1925 (lithographed in blue on the back). See also QUADRILLÉ.

WATERMARK DETECTOR.—A black porcelain slab or metal tray used for examining stamp watermarks with the aid of benzine. See Chapter II.

WHITE BACKS.—The closing down about 1912 of a mill which supplied coloured papers for British colonial stamps led to the temporary use of surface-coloured papers; the stamps printed on these are popularly called " White backs."

WHITE-LINE ENGRAVING.—The line-engraver on metal incises his lines with a burin, and these lines appear in colour in the printed stamp. He cannot engrave " white " lines this way, but when the die is taken up by the transfer roller, lines may be cut by hand or by a rose-engine (see ENGINE-TURNED) on the roller die, and these, transferred to the printing plate, yield white (uninked) lines in the stamp design.

WOODBLOCK, WOODCUT.—Dies engraved in relief on wood have been used in rare instances as hand-stamps to print stamps one at a time. Original dies engraved on wood have more often been used for making stereotype and electrotype clichés or plates for typographic stamp printing, as in the Belgian stamps of 1869–70. See Chapter XV and WOODBLOCK CAPES.

WOODBLOCK CAPES.—The provisional issue of the triangular Cape of Good Hope stamps, made in the colony in 1861, are popularly called "Woodblocks," and their appearance is suggestive of a woodcut origin. The dies were engraved in relief on steel, and the printing was done from stereotypes. Although "woodblock" is not a correct term, the popular name for these stamps is likely to prevail (Plate 2).

WOVE PAPER.—Has a plain, even texture, as commonly used for most books, newspapers, and magazines.

XYLOL.—The spirit in which the best photogravure inks are mixed; stamps printed from such inks should not be immersed in benzine.

ZERO STAMPS.—The numbering of the Spanish stamps at the back (see NUMBERS) starts with six zeros 000,000, but the zero sheet is not normally issued; the issue sheet starts with 000,001. Zero numbers are met with, but rarely in used condition.

ZINCOGRAPHY, ZINCO.—The photo-mechanical process of engraving by etching on sensitised zinc plates in line or half-tone. A zinco is a block or a plate so made.

INDEX